Who's in the Seminary?

Who's in the Seminary?

Roman Catholic Seminarians Today

Martin W. Rovers

Foreword by Andrew Greeley

Who's in the Seminary? Roman Catholic Seminarians Today
   is published by Novalis

Cover design and illustration: D. G. Anderson, ARTEFFECTS

Layout: Gilles Lépine

© 1996, Novalis

Business Office:
   Novalis, 49 Front St. East, 2nd Floor, Toronto, Ontario M5E 1B3

Editorial Office:
   Novalis, 223 Main Street, Ottawa, Ontario KIS 1C4

This book has been published with the help of a grant
   from the Canada Council.

Printed in Canada

Cataloguing in Publication Data

Rovers, Martin W.
      Who's in the seminary?: Roman Catholic
seminarians today

Includes bibliographical references.
ISBN 2-89088-768-5

   1. Seminarians--Canada--Psychology.
2. Seminarians--Canada--Attitudes. 3. Catholic
Church--Canada--Clergy--Psychology. 4. Catholic
Church--Canada--Clergy--Attitudes. 5. Social surveys--
Canada. I. Title.

BX1421.2.R69 1996   305.9'22   C96-900202-5

NOVALIS

Contents

Preface		9
Foreword		11
1	Introduction	13
2	The Theory of Personal Authority, or Maturity	17
	Family–of–Origin Theory	17
	Differentiation of Self	18
	Personal Authority, or Maturity	19
3	Who Are "the Seminarians"?	23
4	Their Theological Attitudes	35
5	The Seminarians' Personal Authority	41
6	Family–of–Origin Factors	45
7	Experiences of Intimacy	53
8	Demographic and Ethnic Factors	63
9	Drawing the Data Together	65
10	Who Do We Have Here? Who Will We Have?	69
	More Maturity in Today's Seminarians	69
	Trends Among Seminarians	70
11	Recruitment of Seminarians	77
	Appealing to an Older Generation	77
	Previously Married Men	79
12	Assessing Seminarians	81

Family–of–Origin Interview	81
Sexual/Social Interview	84
Certainty in Becoming a Priest	85
Guardedness in Assessments	85
Seminarian Formation	87
Personal Authority over the Years	90
The Seminarians' Relationships with Women	92
13 Conclusions, Questions and Recommendations	95
Implications for Future Research	97
Appendix A: The Questionnaire to Seminarians	99
Appendix B: Family–of–Origin Statistics	113
Appendix C: Intimacy Statistics	121
Appendix D: Maturity, Theological Attitude and Age and Regional Factors	127
Appendix E: Maturity, Theological Attitude and Ethnic Factors	129
Glossary	131
References	133

List of Tables and Graphs

1. Diocesan and Religious Priests/Seminarians in Canada 25
2. Candidates for the Priesthood in Canada by Region . 27, 28
3. Seminarians in Canada by Theological Year............. 28, 29
4. Sexual Orientation of Priests and Candidates for the Priesthood................................... 30
5. Age of Seminarians.. 31
6. Seminarians' Involvement in Church–Related Activities Prior to Entering Theology (table only).... 33
7. Theological Attitude Scale Scores of Seminarians..... 36, 37
8. Theological Attitude Scale (Percent Agreeing Strongly or Somewhat) (table only) 38-39
9. Mean Scores on the Personal Authority Scores– As Compared to Other Groups (table only)................ 42
10. Seminarians' Sexual Orientation and Admission of Family Dysfunctions 47, 48
11. Family and Parental Intimacy and Communication Patterns as Experienced by Seminarians (table only).. 49
12. Seminarians' Experiences of Intimacy Prior to Theology 54, 55
13. Best Friends of Roman Catholic Seminarians 56, 57
14. Celibacy and Roman Catholic Seminarians (table only).. 59

Preface

The seminarians of today are the priests of tomorrow's Church. Who are they? What kind of families do they come from? What do they value highly? In general, how do they relate to others?

This is the first national survey of Catholic seminarians in Canada. It is also the first to study seminarians in terms of their family–of–origin, the family in which a person "has his or her beginnings – physiologically, psychically, and emotionally."[1] So this is an exploratory study, and one that I hope will open the door to more intensive studies in the future.

My research covers several areas, but its focus is on the level of *maturity* of Catholic seminarians in Canada. Another way of naming maturity is *personal authority,* and I use these terms interchangeably. I look at the association between numerous family–of–origin, intimacy and demographic factors, on the one hand, and the varying levels of maturity, on the other. I also review the theological attitudes of seminarians today and compare them to the attitudes of seminarians of 10 and 25 years ago.

I am truly thankful to the many people who played a role in my doctoral studies. Thanks is owed to my family, especially my mom, Nel, and my dad, Martin; to my religious community – the Missionary Oblates of Mary Immaculate – for their support and encouragement over the years, and especially in the formation

---

[1] Hovestradt, Anderson, Piercy, Cochran, and Fine 1985, 287.

process. Thanks, too, must be given to the Roman Catholic seminaries and seminarians of Canada for their generous support and honesty.

A heartfelt thanks goes to Dr. Bill Hague and the members of my thesis committee for their guidance, review and support. And more personally, to Bernadette, for encouraging me to begin my doctoral studies.

I dedicate this work to the memory of my two deceased sisters: Maria Rovers, Ph.D., and Nellie Aitken, M.Ed., whose achievements gave me strength and a goal.

Foreword

Typically we who do social research describe our work as preliminary, a modesty which is not only becoming but gives us an opportunity to describe what we want to do next. One may admire the modesty of Martin Rovers and his clarity about what comes next – surely research on seminarians' and priests' relationships with women is of the higher order of importance. Yet it would be a mistake for the reader of this book to think that the modesty, while undoubtedly sincere, is an accurate reflection of Dr. Rovers's accomplishment.

He has answered some very important questions about seminarians:

- They are on the average more mature emotionally than those in comparison groups.
- More of them are homosexual than in the past (though I'm necessarily unsure about that). Nonetheless, despite wild rumours to the contrary, most are not. Indeed, a very able and perceptive seminary rector made an estimate recently which fit perfectly with that of Dr. Rovers.
- Their piety, alas, is alarmingly out of sync with that of other priests and the educated Catholic laity. This could become a very serious problem as the years go on, because the laity, who are already losing respect for priests, may well go into open revolt against them. On the other hand, it may be that the comparison between priests and seminarians is not as appropriate as it might seem. It would be very useful if Dr. Rovers could follow up on

these men after their seminary education is completed and they are ordained. My own research on young priests in the United States suggests that, while on the average they are somewhat more conservative, they are not totally different from their predecessors.

His study of seminarians, therefore, is not only intelligent and professional, it is stimulating and challenging. One hopes that the climate of opinion in the Church on social research is changing, that priests and bishops will no longer dismiss it as having no more value than individual personal experience, and that they will listen closely and carefully to scholars like Dr. Rovers who carefully and responsibly pinpoint both problems and possibilities.

One can always hope.

In any event this study is a superior piece of work. It was a pleasure to serve on Martin Rovers's dissertation committee. I congratulate him on his success and urge him to keep up the good work.

Andrew Greeley
Tucson
January 25, 1996

1

Introduction

Seminarians today are faced with a wide range of life issues that strongly affect their personal development as priests–to–be. The "essential relational challenge of adulthood"[2] is the achievement of *personal authority*, or maturity, which is a proper balance of individuation, on the one hand, and intimacy in relationships with others, on the other. *Individuation* is "an individual's ability to function in an autonomous and self–directed manner without being controlled, impaired, or feeling unduly responsible for significant others."[3] This process of becoming an individual can be impeded in a seminary theological education that frowns on questioning and dissent, and in a Church where obedience is promised to the Bishop.

The other part of the equation, *intimacy,* may be defined as "closeness with distinct boundaries."[4] The development of healthy expressions of intimacy in relationship with those to whom one ministers, and especially with women who make up the majority of Church members, can be encumbered in an all–male seminary, and in a Church where celibacy is required. If, on the one hand, priests are too individuated and lack appropriate intimacy, they tend to be authoritarian and distant, and to proceed blithely with their own agenda. If, on the other hand, they lack

---

[2] Williamson 1991, 3.
[3] Ibid., 275.
[4] Lewis, Beavers, Gossett & Phillips 1976: Williamson 1981, 1982b, 310.

proper individuation but also seek intimacy and connection, they can tend to become insecure or accommodating leaders.

Achieving maturity through balanced individuation and intimacy in relationships is the goal of seminary formation. Indeed, maturity is an essential quality that enhances the sharing of leadership and faith, that encourages the sharing of responsibility equally and mutually by men and women, and that allows one to manage conflict wherever it may arise – in the parish, with the Bishop, and so on. Living the Christian example expected of priests remains the primary goal.

In light of the recent exposure of sexual abuse by priests, the question of seminary formation is a pressing one. In response to this pattern of abuse, the report of the Canadian Conference of Catholic Bishops' Ad Hoc Committee on Sexual Abuse stated: "Steps need to be taken to reassure the faithful that priestly formation programs across the country would be assisted, in every possible way, to foster a human formation that is truly integral and based upon the best resources that can be provided."[5] The fact of sexual abuse, as well as the ordinary issues of priestly relationships, require that the matter of maturity or personal authority be addressed in the formation process of seminarians.

The objectives of my study can be presented in the form of three questions:
1) How does personal authority or maturity of Canadian seminarians as measured by a recognized analytical instrument for family systems[6] compare with that of university students[7] and other groups studied by other researchers?
2) What correlations are there between aspects of the seminarians' families of origin and their experiences of intimacy, on

---

[5] "The Selection and Formation of Candidates for the Priesthood," 1992, 1.

[6] The Personal Authority in the Family System Questionnaire – College Version (PAFS–QVC). This instrument is available from Dr. James H. Bray, Ph.D., Department of Family Medicine, Baylor College of Medicine, 5510 Greenbriar, Houston, Texas, 77005, telephone (713) 798–7751.

[7] The Personal Authority in the Family System Normative Group of university students.

the one hand, and the varying degrees of personal authority or maturity, on the other?

3) What are the theological attitudes of Canadian seminarians today and their experiences of ministry, as compared to those of seminarians studied in 1969, 1971, 1985 and 1987?[8]

This work begins with a discussion of the theory of personal authority, or maturity. I then present the information I gathered from my survey of seminarians as follows:
- a background profile of seminarians;
- their theological attitudes;
- their level of personal authority or maturity; and
- the significance of different factors, including family–of–origin, degree of intimacy, demographics and ethnicity.

The data is presented by means of tables and graphs in the text, while the raw statistical data are included in the appendices. The data is reported with little interpretation or commentary. The possible implications of the results and the author's own commentary are reserved for the concluding chapter.

I hope that this study will contribute to a better understanding of Canadian seminarians today.[9] This in turn may help to improve the formation of future seminarians, our future priests.

---

[8] Studies by Potvin and Suziedelis (1969), Stryckman and Gaudet (1971), Potvin (1985), and Hemrick and Hoge (1987).

[9] There have been numerous studies on the priesthood and the related area of seminary life. Potvin and Suziedelis (1969), Potvin (1985) and Hemrick & Hoge (1987) studied American seminarians and included family demographics and attitudes towards celibacy. Stryckman and Gaudet (1971) identified demographics of seminarians in Canada in conjunction with correlated attitudes. Our study presents an updated profile of Canadian seminarians and looks at implications for the future.

2

The Theory of Personal Authority, or Maturity

How do we understand *maturity* or *personal authority* in relationships? This chapter provides an introduction to the theoretical underpinnings of this study in family–of–origin theory and the concept of personal authority. (Those who wish to know more about the theory per se should consult the works listed in the reference section.)

Family–of–Origin Theory

A family of origin can be understood as the living unit in which a person has his/her beginnings – physiologically, psychically and emotionally, as noted above.[1] Not surprisingly, the theory holds that much of one's current self–image, values, behaviours, attitudes, and relations with others are, in varying degrees, regulated by the experiences of one's family.

Murray Bowen is one of the original thinkers in the field of family systems theory. Bowen (1978) conceptualizes the family

---

[1] The influence of the family upon its members is noted in the theoretical writings of Boszormenyi–Nagy and Spark (1973), Framo (1976, 1981), Bowen (1976, 1978), Kerr and Bowen (1988), and Williamson (1978, 1991), among others.

as an emotional unit, a network of interlocking relationships, best understood when analyzed in terms of more than one generation. "Rather than functioning as autonomous psychological entities, individual family members are inextricably tied in thinking, feeling and behaviour to the family system."[2] Bowen began to observe that family members functioned in reciprocal relationships. He defined such family interaction as an "emotional unit." The term "emotional" refers to everything that guides the individual automatically within an environment or family. Thus family systems theory sees every person as a member of an emotional system or unit.

According to Bowen (1978), the fundamental variable characterizing the quality of family relationships is the level of differentiation that family members achieve. Bowen attributed the variation in an individual's or a family's ability to differentiate to six related factors:

- skill in understanding, identifying and handling issues involving family "triangles" (in which, say, a parent calls on the child to "take sides" against the other parent, or a parent intervenes in a conflict between the child and the other parent);
- the emotional development of the nuclear family;
- the process of family projection (in which parental problems are projected onto a child or onto children);
- the process of multi–generational transmission;
- emotional cut–off (in which close relationships are suddenly broken off by physical or emotional distance);
- sibling position.

Differentiation of Self

As used by Bowen (1978), the term *differentiation* means a life–long process of striving to preserve self in close relationships. It refers to a person's ability to operate in an autonomous manner, without being impaired or feeling overly responsible for significant others. It has less to do with behaviour than with one's

---
   [2]   Goldenberg & Goldenberg 1991, 147.

emotional being. The differentiated person is one who is oriented by principles and can assume responsibility for self.

Kerr wrote in 1984 that "every person has some degree of unresolved emotional attachment to his/her parental family.... [T]his unresolved attachment to family of origin parallels one's level of differentiation of self."[3] Differentiation requires that one make conscious efforts to "de–triangulate" oneself from intense emotional attachments to parents and others in order to reorient relationships in a free and loving manner. The degree to which one is able to orient oneself to others in ways that respect one's individual autonomy, as well as one's intimacy with the other, defines one's capacity to act in a differentiated manner. Thus people will differ from one to another in degree of differentiation.

Bowen (1978) described the *fused* or undifferentiated person as one who operates largely on an emotional level. Fusion or low–level differentiation indicates that someone's beliefs, attitudes, emotions and reactions are governed by the emotional aspects of close relationships and other emotional forces in the environment. Often the person is intent on satisfying his/her needs for togetherness and will comply automatically with his/her particular group. Because of poor self–other boundaries, the fused person is oriented to relationships, to reacting emotionally to the needs of others and to seeking approval from others. Fused people tend either to avoid or to "cut off" close relationships so as not to become automatically "fused" or tied to intense relationships, and to gratify emotional needs.

Personal Authority, or Maturity

Williamson (1991) defines personal authority as a paradox of intimacy: An adult "leaves the parental home psychologically in a complete sense [yet] still belongs emotionally with the family of origin."[4] Williamson integrates Bowen's concept of differentiation with that of intimacy, defining the result as "the ability to be close but at the same time maintain clear boundaries

---

[3] Kerr 1984, 8.
[4] Williamson & Bray 1988, 5.

to the self."⁵ Personal authority and maturity is achieved when one is fully differentiated, and one can then reconnect voluntarily in love and intimacy with members of one's own family, especially parents, and with peers.

Williamson and Bray define personal authority as a set of relational skills that can be observed in family interactions and other important interpersonal relationships. Specifically, they contend that personal authority or maturity is a pattern of abilities:
- to order and direct one's own thoughts and opinions;
- to choose to express or not to express one's thoughts and opinions, regardless of social pressure;
- to make personal judgments and respect them;
- to take responsibility for the totality of one's experience of life;
- to initiate or to receive intimacy voluntarily, in conjunction with the ability to set clear boundaries for the self at will; and
- to experience and to relate to all other persons without exception, including "former parents," as peers in the experience of being human.⁶

The Personal Authority in the Family System Questionnaire – College Version⁷ (PAFS–QCV) is designed to measure key aspects of maturity or personal authority in intergenerational familial relationships. This questionnaire is specifically designed for college–age and unmarried people. It is comprised of seven *scales*, groups of questions designed to elicit responses which can then be graded or measured in terms of various factors of personal and social development. These scales are described by Bray and Harvey (1987) as follows:

1) Intergenerational Intimacy: Intimacy is defined as voluntary closeness with distinct boundaries to the self (Williamson 1981). Closeness without boundaries or closeness that is not voluntary is synonymous with fusion or enmeshment. This scale assesses relationships with parents in terms of satisfac-

---
[5] Ibid., 362.
[6] Williamson & Bray 1984, 168.
[7] Bray, Williamson & Malone 1984; Bray & Harvey 1987.

tion, intimacy, trust and self-disclosure. Examples of items on this scale include: a) "I share my true feelings with my mother/father about the significant events in my life," and b) "I openly show tenderness toward my mother/father." Higher scores indicate more intimacy.

2) Intergenerational Individuation: The items in this scale measure the degree to which a person operates with parents in a fused or individuated way. Examples of items on this scale include: a) "My present–day problems would be fewer or less severe if my parents had acted or behaved differently," and b) "I am usually able to disagree with my parents without losing my temper." Higher scores indicate higher levels of individuation.

3) Intergenerational Intimidation: Items on this scale measure the degree of personal intimidation experienced by an individual in relation to his/her parents or the degree to which an adult yields to the wishes of his/her parents. Examples of items on this scale include: a) "To meet my mother's/father's expectations concerning my appearance (life style, vocation), I feel I must modify my behaviour." Higher scores indicate less intimidation.

4) Intergenerational Triangulation: The items in this scale measure triangulation which tends to cause conflicts between children and their parents. Examples of items on this scale include: a) "How often do you feel compelled to take sides when your parents disagree?" and b) "How often does your mother/father intervene in a disagreement between you and your father/mother?" Higher scores indicate less triangulation.

5) Peer Intimacy: Items on this scale measure intimacy with significant others in a dyadic relationship. Peer intimacy is defined similarly to intergenerational intimacy. Examples of items on this scale include: a) "My significant other and I have mutual respect for each other," and b) "My significant other and I frequently show tenderness to each other." Higher scores indicate greater intimacy.

6) Peer Individuation: Items on this scale indicate the degree to which a person operates in a fused or individuated manner in

a significant dyadic relationship. Individuated, that is, self-governing and self-determined functioning, includes taking responsibility for oneself and not being controlled by a significant peer. Examples of items on this scale include: a) "I get so emotional with my significant other that I cannot think straight," and b) "I feel my significant other says one thing to me and really means another." Higher scores on this scale indicate higher levels of individuation.

7) Personal Authority: This scale measures the number of times conversations have occurred between adult children and their parents which required an intimate interaction and the maintenance of individual stances. Examples of items on this scale include: a) "How comfortable are you in talking to your mother and father about family secrets, both real and imagined, and about skeletons in the family closet?" and b) "How comfortable are you in talking face–to–face to your mother and father to make explicit to them that you are not responsible for his/her survival or happiness in life, and that you are not working to meet goals and achievements in life which have been passed on from them (or prior generations) to you." Higher scores indicate more personal authority on this scale.

In sum, increasing degrees of personal authority or maturity are indicated by higher scores on these scales. Higher scores mean more intimacy and more individuation with parents and peers, less intimidation and less triangulation with parents, and more personal authority. The higher the scores, the greater is one's individuation, and the greater one's ability to be intimate, and consequently to live with more maturity.

3

Who Are "the Seminarians"?

To learn what I wanted to know about the seminarians and personal authority, I sent a questionnaire[8] to the whole population of 455 seminarians – diocesan and religious, French and English – all students in theology and/or the pastoral year of preparation for the priesthood in the Roman Catholic Church in Canada.[9]

---

[8] The questionnaire included many items from those of others: the Personal Authority in the Family System Questionnaire – College Version (PAFS – QVC), parts of the Stryckman and Gaudet (1971), Potvin (1985), and Hemrick & Hoge (1987) studies, and the National Opinion Research Center's study of Catholic Priests in the United States Theological Attitude Scale (NORC 1972). I also used items from "The Selection and Formation of Candidates for the Priesthood," the report presented by the Ad Hoc Committee on Sexual Abuse (1992) of the Canadian Conference of Catholic Bishops. Additional items concerning family demographics, especially in the area of family violence and sexual abuse, were added by the researcher from more recent family studies. Questions about peer intimacy were included after discussion with seminary rectors and other formation personnel. (The rectors and formation personnel were sent copies of the original draft of the pilot study. This informed them of the purpose of the study, and allowed for their comments and input when it came to the final draft.)

[9] Initially, all seminary rectors and the superiors of Religious communities of priests in Canada were sent introductory letters. The purpose was to seek their cooperation with the study and to ask them to report the number of seminarians. Almost all reported back. Those who did not were phoned and the information gathered. Statistics revealed 341 diocesan seminarians and 114 religious seminarians, for a total of 455 seminarians in Canada in 1994.

Two hundred and three questionnaires were returned (a 44.6 return rate).[10] When one considers the very personal nature of the questionnaire, this may be considered a good response.

The data from this survey of seminarians in Canada today are compared in the present study to those from other studies of Catholic seminarians, most notably Potvin and Suziedelis (1969), Potvin (1985), and Hemrick and Hoge (1987).

Of the seminarians who responded to my questionnaire, 72.4% stated that they were studying for the diocesan priesthood and 27.6% stated that they were preparing for priesthood in a religious community. The Canadian Conference of Catholic Bishops statistics on the Church (1989) show that, in 1989, 74.0% of those studying were candidates for the diocesan priesthood, while 26.0% were candidates for the religious priesthood. Potvin (1985) found that 71.7% of those in preparation in the U.S. were candidates for the diocesan priesthood, while 21.7% were candidates for the religious priesthood, and 6.6% were "other."

Results indicate that the percentage of diocesan seminarians continues to increase and that the percentage of religious seminarians continues to decrease. Table 1 compares the results of this survey of seminarians with Canadian Church statistics of priests in Canada.

---

[10] The questionnaire was presented in both English and French to accommodate the language of the individuals answering it. The French translation of the questionnaire was done by two professional translators who work full–time for the Oblate Conference of Canada. This work was then reviewed by two fully bilingual priests who work in seminary formation.

Graph and Table 1
Diocesan and Religious Priests/Seminarians in Canada

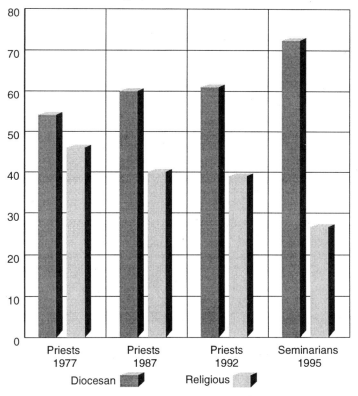

	Priests						Seminarians
Affiliation	1977*	%	1987	%	1992	%	Rovers 1995
Diocesan	7498	(54)	6610	(60)	6456	(61)	(72.4)
Religious	6378	(46)	4435	(40)	4167	(39)	(26.6)
Note: * Statistics of the Catholic Church in Canada, Ottawa: CCCB, 1993.							

When considered by regions in Canada, the sample population from my study compares favourably with Church statistics for 1989 as presented by the Canadian Conference of Catholic Bishops Report (1991). Table 2 suggests that the Quebec – Ontario responses to the research questionnaire are similar to those of the 1989 population. Similarities are also found when the respondent's year of theological study is compared to the entire population. The data are presented in Table 3.

**Graph 2
Candidates for the Priesthood in Canada
by Region**

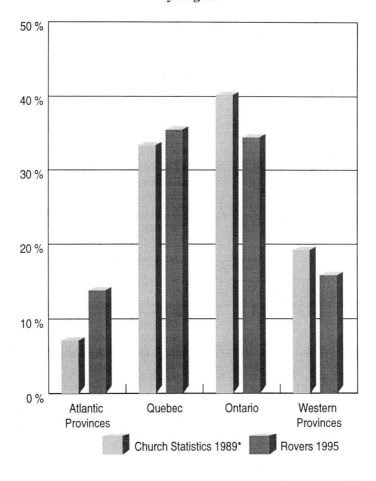

Table 2
Candidates for the Priesthood in Canada by Region

	Church Statistics 1989*	Rovers 1995
Atlantic Provinces	7.1%	13.8%
Quebec	33.4%	35.5%
Ontario	40.2%	34.5%
Western Provinces	19.2%	15.8%

Note. * Statistics of the Catholic Church in Canada, Ottawa: CCCB, 1991.

Graph and Table 3
Seminarians in Canada by Theological Year

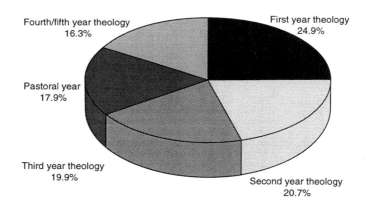

Fourth/fifth year theology 16.3%
First year theology 24.9%
Pastoral year 17.9%
Third year theology 19.9%
Second year theology 20.7%

	Church Statistics 1993 *	Rovers 1995
First year theology	20.0%	24.9%
Second year theology	22.0%	20.7%
Third year theology	19.0%	19.9%
Pastoral year	26.0%	17.9%
Fourth/fifth year theology	13.0%	16.3%
* Unofficial Church statistics gathered from seminary rectors.		

On the question of sexual orientation, the research responses seem in keeping with results of an American study. Murphy (1992) studied Roman Catholic priests, both diocesan and religious, to examine their attitudes and behaviours regarding sexuality, celibacy and relationships. Table 4 displays these comparative data.

Graph and Table 4
Sexual Orientation of Priests and Candidates for the Priesthood

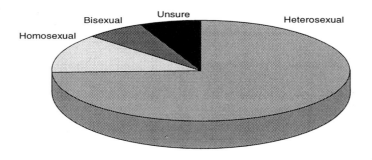

	Murphy 1992[*]	Rovers 1995
Heterosexual	72.2%	74.5%
Homosexual	18.6%	12.5%
Bisexual	9.2%	6.5%
Unsure		6.5%

* Murphy 1992, 133.

The mean age of Canadian seminarians today is 31.4 years. Table 5 compares the age data from three other studies. Whereas in 1966, 72.0% of seminarians were under the age of 25, today 42.3% of seminarians are more than 31 years old. My research shows that the trend toward older seminarians continues.

Graph and Table 5
Age of Seminarians

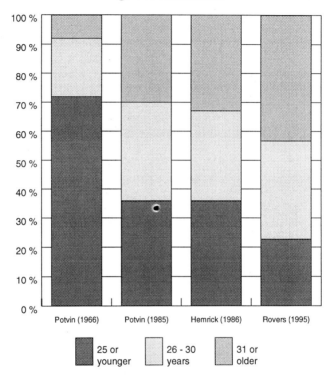

	Potvin (1966)	Potvin (1985)	Hemrick (1986)	Rovers (1995)
25 or younger	72%	36%	36%	22.7%
26 – 30 years	20%	34%	31%	34.0%
31 or older	7%	30%	33%	42.3%
Mean age (years)	25.20	29.55	29.95	31.4

The vast majority of seminarians was born in Canada (86.6%). The second largest group was born in Asia (5.4%), followed by those from Europe (4.3%) and the United States (2.7%).

Canadian seminarians today seem to have been less involved in various community and Church activities prior to entering into theology than the seminarians of 1987. Table 6 compares the percentage of involvement. On the one hand, there appears to have been decreased involvement in Church–related activities such as altar server, eucharistic minister or lector. On the other hand, there has been increased involvement in charismatic groups and Cursillo.

Table 6
Seminarians' Involvement in Church Activities Prior to Entering Theology

	Rovers 1995		Hemrick 1987	
	involved regularly*	involved at all**	involved regularly	involved at all
Altar boy	47%	66%	62%	77%
Eucharistic minister or lector	40%	77%	47%	77%
Boy scout	25%	41%	24%	47%
Working in rectory	19%	45%	25%	51%
Teaching Catholic religion	17%	50%	29%	68%
Engaged in social work	17%	46%	19%	58%
Charismatic group	14%	51%	10%	48%
Member of parish council	10%	27%	10%	24%
Engaged in hospital work	8%	37%	15%	49%
Cursillo	7%	15%	3%	12%

Note: * involved on a regular basis; ** involved regularly, once or twice or on an irregular basis

4

Their Theological Attitudes

My questionnaire surveyed the theological attitudes of seminarians, and their responses were quantified. These are presented in Table 7, the Theological Attitude Scale Scores for Seminarians. The mean Theological Attitude Scale score for Roman Catholic Seminarians in Canada today is 37.2 as compared with 39.8 for seminarians in 1985 (Potvin 1985). Since lower scores indicate more traditional theological attitudes and higher scores indicate more modern theological attitudes, seminarians today are significantly more traditional than their counterparts of only ten years ago.

The difference between diocesan and religious seminarians also approaches statistical significance, and therefore may be considered true. Religious seminarians (mean = 38.6) tend to be more modern in their theological attitude than their diocesan counterparts (mean = 36.7). When age is considered, the difference today between the theological attitudes of diocesan and religious seminarians is negligible, whereas Potvin reported that the difference in 1985 was statistically significant.

Graph 7
Theological Attitude Scale Scores of Seminarians

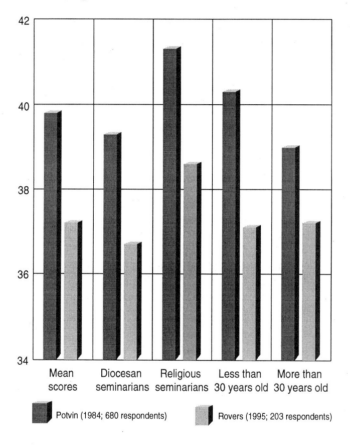

(Higher scores indicate more modern theological attitudes.)

Table 7
Theological Attitude Scale Scores of Seminarians

	Potvin (1984) N= 680	Rovers (1995) N= 203
Mean scores	39.8	37.2
Diocesan seminarians	39.3	36.7
Religious seminarians	41.3	38.6
Less than 30 years old	40.3	37.1
More than 30 years old	39.0	37.2
Note: * Higher scores = more modern theological attitude Lower scores = more traditional theological attitude Range is from 12 (traditional) to 60 (modern)		

Table 8 (next page) presents the percentage agreeing "strongly" or "somewhat" with the traditional or modern items on the Theological Attitude Scale. This is compared to the NORC (1972) study of young priests in the United States, ages 26–35, as well as the Potvin (1985) study of American seminarians in 1985. Since many of the young priests of 1970 would have been seminarians in the late 1960s, some comparative analysis is possible.

Table 8
Theological Attitude Scale
(Percent Agreeing Strongly or Somewhat)

Items	1970* NORC	1985 Potvin	1995 Rovers
M** Today's Christians must emphasize more than ever openness to the Spirit rather than dependence upon traditional ecclesiastical structures.	89	78	27.5
M For me, God is found principally in my relationship with people.	78	78	23.8
M Salvation is total liberation from both individual and collective sin, from injustice and inhuman conditions in the here and now.	NA***	65	26.9
M Faith is primarily an encounter with God in Jesus Christ, rather than an assent to a coherent set of defined truths.	92	86	10.4
M There are times when a person has to obey his or her personal conscience rather than the Church's Teaching.	80	84	21.8
M When I experience moments of deep communication and union with other persons, these sometimes strike me as a taste of what Heaven might be like.	81	75	12.4
T** I think of God primarily as the Supreme Being, immutable, all-powerful, and the Creator of the Universe.	31	59	62.7
T Salvation is mainly liberation from sin. It has to do with the wellbeing of souls and their preparation for eternal life.	NA***	63	65.3

Note * From NORC 1972, 83–98, Ages 26–35
    ** M = Modern item; T = Traditional item
    *** NA = not asked

Items	1970* NORC	1985 Potvin	1995 Rovers
T I think of Jesus as the God who humbled himself by becoming man and dying for my sins.	75	83	69.4
T The primary task of the Church is to encourage its members to live the Christian life, rather than to try to reform the world.	29	53	64.2
T A Christian should primarily be concerned with the salvation of his or her own soul; then he or she should be concerned with helping others.	22	26	26.4
T The important thing to stress when teaching about Jesus is that He is truly God, and therefore adoration should be directed toward Him.	NA***	42	51.3
Note * From NORC 1972, 83–98, Ages 26–35 ** M = Modern item; T = Traditional item *** NA = not asked			

From this data we can see that seminarians today are more traditional and less modern than seminarians in the U.S. in 1985. The seminarians of 1985 also appear to be more traditional and less modern than their counterparts of the late 1960s. In short, there emerges a movement in the direction of traditional theological attitudes in the Roman Catholic priesthood over the past thirty years. More seminarians today agreed with the traditional items, and fewer agreed with the modern items. The one exception is the item: "I think of Jesus as the God who humbled himself by becoming man and dying for my sins." Results indicate that 69.4% of seminarians today agree with this item, compared to 83% in 1984 and 75% of young priests in 1970.

5

The Seminarians' Personal Authority

Personal authority or maturity scores were computed for Roman Catholic seminarians in Canada. The results are presented in Table 9. Comparison is made to the scores of the normative group (university students) and to two other studies. With the exception of "intergenerational intimacy," all other maturity scores of seminarians in Canada are significantly higher than the scores of the normative group of men. In other words, seminarians are found to be "more mature" than the other groups.[11]

---

[11] A similar pattern emerges when seminarians' scores are compared to those of the normative group of women, with two exceptions: 1) the normative group of women scored significantly higher than the seminarians on the intergenerational intimacy scale, indicating better ability to be intimate with parents than the seminarians; and 2) no significant difference was found between the normative group of women and seminarians on the peer intimacy scale. When we compare the scores of seminarians on intergenerational individuation and intergenerational triangulation to those of Kinner's (1990) study of male university students, no significant differences are found.

42 WHO'S IN THE SEMINARY?

Table 9
Mean Personal Authority Scores of Seminarians as Compared to Other Groups

	Normative Group	Kinner	Dinunzio	Rovers
	1987 University Students	1990 University Students	1992 Senior Managers	1995 Catholic Seminarians
	Men/Women Age: 20	Men 25	Men/ Women 43	Men 31.4
Intergenerational Intimacy	89.4	93.2		90.4
Intergenerational Individuation	30.2	30.1	32.7	32.4
Intergenerational Intimidation	17.6	17.8		35.9
Intergenerational Triangulation	19.3	18.7	32.6	32.2
Peer Intimacy	44.4	47.2		46.5
Peer Individuation	29.5	29.9		32.7
Personal Authority	41.0	43.8	53.4	45.5

Note. Higher scores indicate more intergenerational intimacy; more intergenerational individuation; less intergenerational intimidation; less intergenerational triangulation; more peer intimacy; more peer individuation; more personal authority.

There are glaring differences between the mean intergenerational intimidation scores of seminarians (35.9) and those of the normative group of men (17.6), and between the mean intergenerational triangulation scores of seminarians (32.2) and those of the normative group of men (19.3). Yet this may be due to the age of the seminarians: when the mean intergenerational triangulation scores of seminarians (32.2) are compared to those in Kinner's study of older university students (32.6), no significant difference is found. As the average age of the normative group of men was 20 years, and that of Kinner's group was 25 years, the substantial differences between seminarians and the normative group may be due to age and maturation.

The same pattern can be seen when mean personal authority scale scores are reviewed. When personal authority scores of seminarians (mean = 45.5) are compared to those of middle and senior management personnel (mean = 53.4) studied by Dinunzio (1992), a significant difference is found. Their scores indicate that the managers are "more mature" than the seminarians, but the managers are also significantly older – 43.0 years on average, compared to the seminarians' 31.4 years. Williamson (1991) may well be right in his claim that the task of developing personal authority, and therefore maturity, begins in earnest in the fourth decade of life.

6

Family-of-Origin Factors

Catholic seminarians come from larger families than the Canadian average. Their families of origin average 4.8 children, as compared to an average of 3.1 children per Canadian family according to Statistics Canada (1991). "Only children" make up 3.0% of the seminary population, while firstborns account for 27.9%, and youngest children account for 22.9%. The percentages are compatible with Potvin's (1985) findings of "only children" (3.7%), firstborn children (27.6%) and youngest children (17.2%).

Family religious affiliation, not surprisingly, is predominantly Catholic. Seminarians whose parents are both Catholic make up 89.7% of the seminarian population. This percentage increases to 96.1% when at least one of the parents is Catholic. Practice of the faith in the family was also studied. More than 87% of seminarians state that they come from homes where faith was practised strongly (Sunday mass, prayer and talking about faith) or moderately (Sunday mass and occasional prayer). Faith practice decreased just slightly (85%) for seminarians after they left home.

Twelve percent of seminarians have experienced separation, divorce or remarriage by parents. Another 19% have lost one parent or both in death. Sixty-nine percent come from families in which there have been no divorces or deaths.

Family dysfunction, with its many faces, is also part of the life of today's seminarian. Seminarians reported the following significant family dysfunctions (percentage of occurrence): alcoholic father (23%); depressed father (11%); addicted father (3%); dysfunctional father other than the above (7%); alcoholic mother (2%); depressed mother (15%); addicted mother (0%); dysfunctional mother other than the above (3%); alcoholic sibling (14%); depressed sibling (14%); addicted sibling (7%); witnessed family violence (26%); victim of family violence (19%); victim of sexual abuse within the family (3%); victim of sexual abuse outside the family (8%).

For the survey questions, family violence was defined as "emotional or physical violence between parents, or between parents and children, or among children."[12] Sexual abuse was defined as "inappropriately exposed or subjected to sexual contact, activity or behaviour."[13] Drawing comparisons to the Canadian population is difficult because there are few studies that have accurately established the rate of these family dysfunctions. In the area of sexual abuse, however, the *Report of the Badgley Committee of Sexual Offenses Against Children* (1984) suggests that 10% of men have experienced sexual abuse either within or outside the family. Lew (1988) believes that it is more like 12–15% of the male population.

When some family dysfunctions are observed in relation to sexual orientation, a more revealing pattern seems to emerge. Seminarians who indicated their sexual orientation to be heterosexual or homosexual showed lower percentages of family dysfunctions. Seminarians who indicated their sexual orientation to be bi–sexual, or were unsure of their orientation, indicated a greater percentage of most family dysfunctions. Table 10 presents these data.

---

[12] Office for the Prevention of Family Violence, Edmonton, Alberta.
[13] Ibid.

Graph 10
Seminarians' Sexual Orientation and Admission of Family Dysfunction

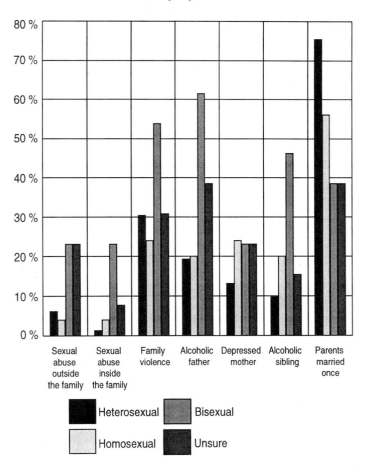

Table 10
Seminarians' Sexual Orientation and Admission of Family Dysfunction

	Hetero-sexual	Homosexual	Bi-sexual	Unsure
Family Dysfunction				
Sexual abuse outside the family	6.1%	4.0%	23.1%	23.1%
Sexual abuse inside the family	1.3%	4.0%	23.1%	7.7%
Family violence	30.4%	24.0%	53.8%	30.8%
Alcoholic father	19.3%	20.0%	61.5%	38.5%
Depressed mother	13.1%	24.0%	23.1%	23.1%
Alcoholic sibling	9.7%	20.0%	46.2%	15.4%
Parents married once	75.5%	56.0%	38.5%	38.5%

Our study also examined family and parental intimacy and patterns of communication. Today's seminarians did not see their family experiences in as favourable a light as did the seminarians of 1985. Table 11 (next page) compares the results of this study to those of Potvin (1985). Results suggest that seminarians are not as happy today as before. They also report more unhealthy patterns in parental communication.

Table 11
Family and Parental Intimacy and Communication Patterns as Experienced by Seminarians

	Rovers 1995		Potvin 1985	
	True	False	True	False
1) Compared to others, our family is (was) very closely knit.	73.9%	26.1%	77.7%	22.3%
2) I do not think my parents are (were) as compatible as most.	30.2%	69.8%	23.1%	76.9%
3) My parents do not (did not) talk to each other enough.	36.5%	63.5%	31.3%	68.7%
4) My parents really love (loved) each other.	80.7%	19.3%	88.8%	11.2%
5) There are things I would liked to have changed about my family.	63.1%	36.9%	74.3%	25.7%
6) I was not happy at home.	21.3%	78.7%	15.5%	84.5%
7) My parents disagreed on many things.	29.9%	70.1%	28.6%	71.4%
8) My parents often quarrelled at home.	26.8%	73.2%	27.2%	72.8%

Appendix B presents the sixteen family–of–origin factors found to be statistically different in relationship to personal authority scores and theological attitude scores. Most family–of–origin factors seem to have affected more than one scale or area of relationship with parents and family.

Practice of faith in the family has a strong positive influence on the level of intergenerational intimacy experienced by seminarians. Indeed, it seems that intergenerational intimacy increases as practice of faith in the family increases. A significant difference exists between strong practice of family faith (mean = 96.0) and little practice of family faith (mean = 76.9). To put this another way: the family that prays together, stays together, or at least has more intergenerational intimacy.

Similarly, those whose parents were married tended to have higher intergenerational intimacy scores. Seminarians who have one parent score much lower and generally at the same level of intergenerational intimacy.

A significant difference exists between seminarians whose parents were married (mean = 94.0), and those whose parents were separated/divorced (mean = 79.8) or widowed (mean = 78.2). Having noted earlier that 69% of seminarians come from intact families, some weight can be given to that old adage that priestly vocations come from intact Catholic families.

Other observations: parental or sibling dysfunctions, such as alcoholism, depression or addiction, reduced intergenerational intimacy and individuation, increased intergenerational intimidation and triangulation, and lowered personal authority in all cases that were shown to be statistically significant. This might seem to be a given in any family, but it is interesting to see such a clear pattern. Sibling addiction also appeared to be a factor in a more modern theological attitude score.

The same pattern can be found with seminarians who were victims of family violence. Again, intergenerational intimacy and individuation decreased, and intergenerational intimidation and triangulation increased in families of seminarians where violence was present. In other words, family violence tends to leave people more immature.

For seminarians who were sexually abused outside the family, and especially for those who were victims inside the family, peer intimacy scores increased. This indicated a greater ability to be intimate with others. At first, these results may seem somewhat surprising in that the experience of abuse seems to improve maturity, at least among peers. It may be that those abused turned to their peers for support, and developed the capacity for intimacy from necessity. Not surprisingly, intimacy with parents is often decreased owing to sexual abuse, because sexual abuse is usually by an adult.

7

Experiences of Intimacy

Our study asked about experiences of intimacy before priests–to–be entered the seminary. The results were as follows: 88.5% of seminarians stated that they had been in love; 82.7% of seminarians said that they had dated prior to entering the seminary; and 68.0% said that they had dated one person steadily for more than three months. Among Canadian seminarians, 64.2% stated that they had considered marriage at some point before entering the seminary. Three percent of seminarians had been previously married.

Table 12 compares these statistics with Potvin (1985). The results: Canadian seminarians today seem to have less experience in all areas of intimacy than did their American counterparts of 1984.

Graph 12
Seminarians' Experiences of Intimacy
Prior to Theology

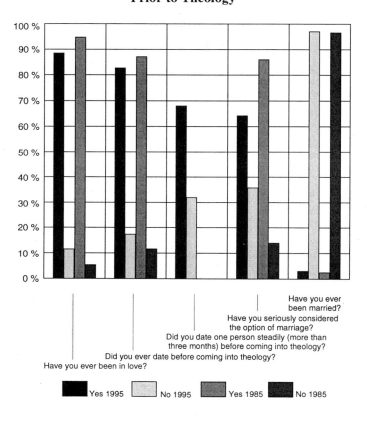

Table 12
Seminarians' Experiences of Intimacy
Prior to Theology

	Rovers 1995		Potvin 1985	
	Yes	No	Yes	No
1) Have you ever been in love?	88.5%	11.5%	94.7%	5.3%
2) Did you ever date before coming into theology?	82.7%	17.3%	87.1%*	11.6%
3) Did you date one person steadily (more than three months) before coming into theology?	68.0%	32.0%	**	**
4) Have you seriously considered the option of marriage?	64.2%	35.8%	86.0%	14.0%
5) Have you ever been married?	3.0%	97.0%	2.5%*	96.6%
Note: * the total of the two columns is less than 100% because some did not answer; ** these questions were not asked by Potvin				

Seminarians' Experiences of Intimacy
Prior to Theology

When asked with whom they feel that they can be most intimate, the largest percentage (34.3%) of seminarians said Jesus or God. Table 13 presents all of the findings. We notice that for all groups of seminarians, women rated third behind Jesus/God and other men. When age is considered, the ranking changes somewhat: for older seminarians, Jesus or God takes on increased importance. Under the category "other," many seminarians wrote that they would feel most intimate with a married couple or with both men and women.

Graph 13
Best Friends of Roman Catholic Seminarians

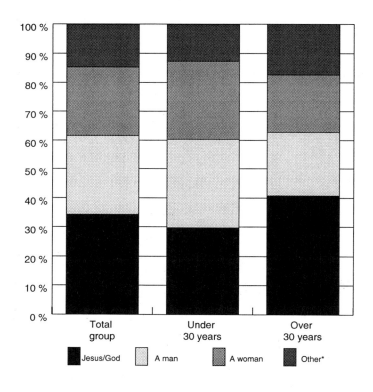

Table 13
Best Friends of Roman Catholic Seminarians

	Total group	Under 30 years	Over 30 years
My best friend is			
Jesus/God	34.3%	29.7%	40.7%
A man	27.3%	30.6%	22.1%
A woman	23.7%	27.0%	19.8%
Other*	14.6%	12.6%	17.4%
Note: * Many responses in this section indicated married couples or both men and women.			

Seminarians were also asked what were the main factors that caused them to consider becoming a priest in the Church today. They offered a number of reasons: an inner call (46%) was the reason most commonly given, followed by the desire to help others (16%), the example of another priest (15%), prior involvement in Church activities (8%), a retreat or discernment experience (7%), the encouragement of parents (3%) and the example of religious brothers and sisters (2%).[1]

Seminarians stated that they were "absolutely sure" (29%) or "sure" (54%) of their desire to become a priest. Only 17% were "unsure" or "very unsure" of their decision.

Diocesan priests make a promise of celibacy when they are ordained. This is in accord with the rule of the Church that Roman Catholic priests cannot be married. Canadian seminarians today are more definite about the place of this promise of celibacy and less willing to do away with it: 56.9% stated that the promise of celibacy should be a perpetual promise, while only 20.3% stated that there should be no promise at all. In contrast,

---

[1] All these responses are within 2% of results found by Potvin (1985).

Potvin (1985) found that 44.3% stated their belief in a perpetual promise, and 28.2% stated that there should be no promise at all. Seminarians were also asked if they would seriously consider marriage if the Church were to permit it. Table 14 compares their responses to those found by Potvin (1985). Fewer seminarians today (17.7%) would definitely or probably consider marrying than seminarians in 1985 (30.1%). Furthermore, a larger percentage of seminarians today (63.6%) would probably or definitely not consider marrying today as compared with 58.0% in 1985. Seminarians in Canada today appear more definite about not entering into marriage, and much less likely to do so, even if permitted, than were their American counterparts of 1985.

Table 14
Celibacy and Roman Catholic Seminarians

	Rovers 1995	Potvin 1985
Consider Marrying		
Definitely would	5.4%	9.1%
Probably would	12.3%	21.0%
Don't know	11.9%	18.2%
Probably not	42.9%	39.9%
Definitely not	20.7%	18.1%

Appendix C presents the personal authority scores for intimacy factors found to be statistically significant. On the intergenerational intimacy scale, heterosexual seminarians (mean = 92.4) indicate a more intimate relationship with their parents than do homosexual seminarians (mean = 86.4). Seminarians who indicated a sexual orientation as bi–sexual (mean = 81.5) or stated that they were unsure about their sexual orientation (mean = 83.4) scored lower on intimacy with their parents.

Homosexual seminarians seem to have a significantly more modern theological attitude (mean score = 41.0) than heterosexual seminarians (mean score = 36.3).

For the most part, seminarians who have been in love, have considered marriage, or who have dated at all or dated steadily for at least three months prior to entry into theology, scored higher on peer intimacy and/or peer individuation than seminarians who did none of the above. They also scored higher on personal authority. In other words, these experiences seemed to have been positive for these seminarians. However, since higher scores indicate less triangulation, seminarians who considered marriage prior to theology (31.7) indicated that they were more triangulated with their parents than those who did not consider marriage (33.3). They also scored as more "traditional" in theological attitudes.

Seminarians who had been married before theology indicated that they were more free from intergenerational intimidation.

Best friends of Catholic seminarians were listed as either men, women, Jesus/God or "other." Under the category of "other," many seminarians put both men and women or a married couple. Seminarians whose best friend was another man, Jesus or God, or "other" scored higher on the intergenerational triangulation scale, indicating less triangulation with their parents. By contrast, seminarians who preferred a woman as best friend seemed to be more triangulated with their parents, taking sides with one against another. In terms of intergenerational triangulation, one finds a significant difference between seminarians whose best friend was a woman (mean = 29.1) and those whose best friend was a man (mean = 33.0); also between seminarians whose best friend was a woman (mean = 29.1) and those whose best friend was Jesus or God (mean = 32.8). Seminarians whose best friend is a man and those whose best friend is God or Jesus scored almost the same on the intergenerational intimacy scale.

On the theological attitude scale, significant differences can be seen between seminarians whose best friend was Jesus or God (mean = 34.1), on the one hand, and those whose best friend was a man (mean = 37.6), a woman (mean = 39.3), or "other" (mean = 39.4), on the other hand. In other words, seminarians whose best friend was Jesus or God were significantly more traditional theologically than all three other groups.

The longer that seminarians have had their best friend, the more intimate and individuated they appear to be, and the less they indicate triangulation with their parents. Indeed, longer friendships may be seen as a healthy factor in the lives of Roman Catholic seminarians.

Scores on the intergenerational triangulation scale were found to differ significantly when consideration was given to those with whom seminarians were able to be most intimate: those seminarians who are most intimate with another man scored a mean of 33.5, while those who are most intimate with a woman had a mean score of 30.2. In other words, seminarians who were most intimate with a woman were more triangulated with parents than seminarians who were most intimate with a man. When asked with whom seminarians feel most intimate, there are notable differences in scores for intergenerational intimidation between seminarians who feel most intimate with another seminarian (mean = 83.2), those who feel most intimate with Jesus or God (mean = 93.2) and those who feel most intimate with mom or dad (mean = 101.0). Furthermore, one can observe significant differences in personal authority between seminarians who feel most intimate with another seminarian (mean = 41.5), those who feel most intimate with a friend (mean = 46.7), and those who feel most intimate with Jesus/God (mean = 46.9). In short, seminarians who feel most intimate with other seminarians seemed to exhibit less intimacy with parents and less personal authority.

Seminarians were also asked how decisive they thought their decision was to become a priest. Results indicated that the more decisive seminarians were about their decision, the higher they scored on intergenerational and peer intimacy and individuation, and the lower they scored on intergenerational intimidation. Or, put the other way, as seminarians stated more uncertainty about their decisions to become priests, their levels of intimacy and individuation in regard to both parents and peers decreased.

Those seminarians who believed that their promise of celibacy should be kept forever scored highest on intergenerational intimacy. They also indicated less intimidation with parents. Those who indicated a "Don't know" scored lowest. On the intergenerational intimacy scale, there is a significant difference between those seminarians who professed "Don't know" (mean = 81.6) and those who professed a perpetual vow (mean = 94.0). On the intergenerational intimidation scale, a significant difference exists between those seminarians who professed "Don't know" (mean = 33.5) and those who professed a perpetual vow (mean = 36.6). On the theological attitude scale, we see a significant difference in attitude between those seminarians who professed "Don't know" (mean = 38.5) and "no promise" (mean = 42.6) and those who professed a perpetual vow (mean = 35.0). Finally, seminarians who indicated a perpetual promise in accord with the current rules of the Church indicated that they were most traditional in their theological attitudes.

8

Demographic and Ethnic Factors

Few demographic factors were found to be significant in this study. Still, scores on intergenerational triangulation were found to differ significantly when age was considered. The group of seminarians was divided into two groups according to age, those less than 30 years old and those over 30. The older seminarians reported less intergenerational triangulation (mean = 33.7) compared to the younger group (mean = 32.2). (See Appendix D for the data.)

Scores on peer individuation were found to differ significantly when the region from which seminarians came was considered. Significant differences exist between seminarians from Quebec (mean = 30.7) and seminarians from the Maritimes (mean = 34.4), and between seminarians from Quebec (mean = 30.7) and seminarians from Ontario (mean = 34.0).

Scores on the Theological Attitude Scale were also found to differ significantly when the seminarian's region was considered. A notable difference exists between seminarians from Quebec (mean = 39.7) and Ontario (mean = 35.5) and seminarians from Quebec (mean = 39.7) and the Western provinces (mean = 35.6). Quebec seminarians tended to be more modern in their theological attitude than those in the rest of Canada.

Theological Attitude Scale scores also differed significantly when the theological year of the seminarian was considered. Results indicate a significant difference between first–year seminarians (mean = 35.2) and pastoral–year seminarians (mean = 40.0). Seminarians tended to become more modern in theological attitude during these first few years of seminary training.

A number of significant differences were found when ethnic factors were taken into consideration. Appendix E presents the scale scores for personal authority and theological attitude for the different ethnic groups of seminarians. Statistically significant differences were found on all scales except for two. On the intergenerational individuation scale, one observes a significant difference between seminarians whose ethnic background is "Other" (mean = 35.6), English Canadian (mean = 33.2), and French Canadian (mean = 33.2), and seminarians whose ethnic background is Asian (mean = 27.3). Asian seminarians appeared to have less ability to operate as individuals. On the personal authority scale, a significant difference exists between seminarians whose ethnic background is French Canadian (mean = 47.2) and those whose ethnic background is Asian (mean = 35.3). Asian seminarians seem to exhibit less maturity as measured by this personal authority scale. On the peer individuation scale, a significant difference also exists between seminarians whose ethnic background is European (mean = 35.6) and those whose ethnic background is French Canadian (mean = 31.8). European seminarians exhibit more individuation in relation to their peers and friends, while French Canadian seminarians seemed less able to be their own persons with peers.

9

Drawing the Data Together

Personal authority, according to Williamson (1991), is defined as the ability to maximize individuation and intimacy with parents and peers while minimizing intimidation and triangulation. When personal authority scale scores are taken individually, specific geographical, ethnic, family–of–origin and intimacy factors can be seen to interact significantly with these variables.

The first four scales of the Personal Authority Questionnaire for college students concern the relationship to parents. According to Williamson (1991), there is a paradox in this relationship: one must leave the parental home in a very complete sense but still belong emotionally to the family–of–origin. A chief task of adult life is resolving intergenerational issues like intimacy, individuation, intimidation and triangulation. Experiences within the family–of–origin and experiences of intimacy have a strong impact upon the development of that adult life. It is Williamson's contention that the way in which one finally resolves the issue of relationship to the members of one's family of origin, especially father and mother, will determine how one handles all subsequent intimate relationships.

Intergenerational intimacy has been defined as the ability to be close, honest and loving to parents without undue enmeshment. The vast majority of factors that contribute to, or take away from, intimacy with parents are family–of–origin factors. Our data show that intergenerational intimacy was higher where the family was intact, and that it was enhanced by the faith practices of the family. It was also enhanced by the certainty of the seminarians that their choice of the priesthood was right, or by their confidence in the perpetual nature of their vows. By contrast, intergenerational intimacy was lowered where they experienced any of the elements of a dysfunctional family, such as alcoholism, depression, addiction or family violence.

Intergenerational individuation was defined as the ability to function in an autonomous and self–directed manner without being controlled, impaired or feeling unduly responsible for significant others. Most of the factors that decrease individuation were from family dysfunctions. Individuation was enhanced by long–term friendships and certainty about priesthood. Asian seminarians scored significantly lower on the intergenerational individuation scale.

Intergenerational intimidation has been defined as the degree to which an individual yields to the wishes of his or her parents. Intimidation was decreased by intact families and a sense of certainty about priesthood or vows. Intergenerational intimidation was increased by experiences of family dysfunction, especially family violence.

Intergenerational triangulation was defined as being caught up in conflict between one's parents. Factors that decreased triangulation included older age, previous marriage, longer length of friendship and being of Canadian or European descent. Factors that correlated with greater intergenerational triangulation included being of Asian descent, family dysfunctions, intimacy with a woman and consideration of marriage prior to theology.

Peer intimacy has been defined as voluntary closeness to significant others in one's life, combined with distinct boundaries between oneself and them. French Canadians and Europeans indicated higher intimacy with peers, while Asians, Italians and English Canadians indicated less intimacy. Peer intimacy was enhanced by having been in love, by having dated, and by certainty about becoming a priest. The research indicated that experiences of being sexually abused outside the family also increased peer intimacy scores. Peer intimacy scores were lower for those who indicated a family with a dysfunctional mother.

Peer individuation was defined as the degree to which a person operates in an individuated manner, or alternatively, a fused manner, with significant others in his or her life. Seminarians of European descent scored highest on peer individuation, while French Canadians scored lowest. Peer individuation was greater in those who dated prior to theology and in those who were certain about their decision to become priests.

Personal authority has been described as the ability to balance intimacy and individuation with parents and peers while avoiding triangles and minimizing intimidation. French Canadians indicated higher levels of personal authority while Asians scored lowest. Personal authority was enhanced by experiences of being in love, of dating, of considering marriage, and of feeling intimate with parents, with Jesus or God, or with friends outside the seminary. Personal authority was lower for those who experienced a dysfunctional father or mother and for those whose friends were inside the seminary or whose friends were siblings.

On the Theological Attitude Scale, seminarians today seemed to be more traditional and less modern than seminarians 10 and 30 years ago. Bi-sexual and heterosexual seminarians were most traditional, as were seminarians who considered their best friend to be Jesus or God, or who indicated a preference for a perpetual promise of celibacy. Seminarians with more modern theological attitudes included homosexuals, those with an addicted sibling, those who did not consider marriage, and those who professed no vow of celibacy at all.

10

Who Do We Have Here? Who Will We Have?

The purpose of this research was to determine the degrees of personal authority, or maturity, among Roman Catholic seminarians in Canada and to investigate common factors, especially in their families of origin and in their experiences of intimacy, that correlate with the various levels of maturity.

This was an exploratory study. It included both a survey of Catholic seminarians in Canada today and an investigation into family–of–origin dynamics, especially the achievement of personal authority (defined as the balancing of individuation and intimacy). Since the study was exploratory, the following discussion will attempt to draw out implications for the present state of seminarians in Canada today and suggest some directions for future research and formation. Our hope is that this discussion will open the door to ongoing dialogue and review by the Church.

More Maturity in Today's Seminarians

The first research question asked how the maturity or personal authority of Canadian seminarians compared with that of the normative group of university students and with other groups studied by other researchers. The finding: seminarians are significantly more mature when compared to the normative group of men. They indicated significantly more individuation from parents, less triangulation with parents and less intimidation by them, and more intimacy and individuation with peers. Seminarians score a little bit better and sometimes substantially better, and no worse. However, when compared to older university students studied by Kinner (1990), or middle management people studied by Dinunzio (1992), seminarians' scores were similar or less. One might conclude that seminarians are as mature as one should expect of men their age.

Trends Among Seminarians

Another goal of this study was to assess the theological attitudes and experiences of ministry of Canadian seminarians, and to compare these to the attitudes and experiences of seminarians studied by other researchers. Here one can see certain trends: more traditional theological attitudes; more diocesan and fewer religious seminarians and priests; regional shifts in the priest population; and a more homosexual priesthood.

Toward Traditional Theological Attitudes

Table 7 (page 37) presents the results of the Theological Attitude Scale for seminarians today. The trend is in the direction of more traditional theological attitudes, a trend that has been underway for the last twenty–five years. Young and Schoenherr (1992) reviewed the data from the 1984 survey of American seminarians and reaffirmed the findings of that study, which concluded that there would be an increasingly traditional clergy within the Church in the years to come. Their analysis was based upon the increasing age of priests throughout the Church and upon the growing conservatism in younger priests. Unlike Potvin (1985), who found younger seminarians to be more modern in their theological attitude, the current study suggests that this distinction has vanished, and that younger seminarians are now the more traditional ones, though the difference in scores is small.

This shift to a more traditional theological attitude in seminarians and priests might be in keeping with McBrien's assertion that "the fundamental conflict in the church today is [not] between the left and the right, [but] . . . between the center and the right."[2] McBrien seems to suggest that the left has already been nudged out, or has consciously left the Church, leaving the right and the centre to debate theology. Of course, one might need to ask whether the left was forced out of the Church, or was losing the debate and simply withdrew, leaving the right and centre to continue.

This trend toward more traditional theological attitudes affects numerous other issues dealt with in this discussion section. Those holding a more traditional theology are unwilling to consider the ordination of women, expect obedience from those in the priesthood, and have referred to homosexuality as an "objective disorder" (Letter of the Doctrinal Congregation to the Bishops 1986).

Table 8 (page 38) presents the results of the individual questions of the Theological Attitude Scale and compares these results to Potvin (1985) and the NORC study (1970). The findings suggest that seminarians today agree less with the "modern" items on the Theological Attitude Scale, and agree more with the "traditional" items on the scale. One can observe the development of this trend over the past twenty–five years. What seems surprising is that the percentages of agreement with the traditional items are only somewhat increased compared to studies of 1970 and 1985. However, the percentage of agreement with the modern items has decreased substantially. Seminarians today are unable to give as much support to modern theological statements as seminarians in the past. It seems, then, that seminarians today are only somewhat more traditional and a whole lot less modern than their counterparts of the past.

One interpretation of these findings is that the modern items on the Theological Attitude Scale no longer represent an acceptable and clear theological position. On the questionnaire, many seminarians wrote comments to the effect that it is not an either/or item for them, but a both/and item. The items on the Theological Attitude Scale seem to be too blunt and clear–cut and thus inappropriate for today. Perhaps theological thinking and society in general have become more complex and interwoven over these

---

[2] McBrien 1992, 81.

twenty–five years. If this is true, however, why was there not a corresponding significant decrease in agreement with the traditional items on the scale? For whatever reason, the traditional items were not seen to be as black and white, and were seen to be more acceptable. Perhaps the Theological Attitude Scale is no longer an accurate instrument for measuring theological attitudes and a new approach is needed. As McBrien (1992) suggested, the decreased agreement with the modern theological items, which once may have represented or described the far left in the Church, is a concrete demonstration that those very people are less likely to have remained in the Church today. As they continue to leave the Church, so too, any agreement with or consent to modern theological items will continue to decrease.

That there is a trend toward the traditional in theological attitudes may help us identify and understand certain troubles in the Church today, and lead us to wonder about the future. What will the leadership of the future Church be like when it is under the direction of these more traditionally minded men? What leadership style will they have? What theologies and religious practice will be presented to the laity?

Toward the Diocesan Priesthood

There is a continued trend toward the diocesan priesthood and away from the religious priesthood. Table 1 (page 25) presents these results. Whereas in 1977 the diocesan (54%) and religious (46%) composition of priests in Canada was fairly equal, the trend over the past twenty–five years has been strongly in the direction of diocesan priesthood (72.4%) and away from religious priesthood (26.6%).

Several reasons may be noted for this changing trend. In the review of theological attitudes, it was noted that seminarians overall have been moving in the direction of more traditional theological attitudes. Research has shown that diocesan seminarians have been more traditional than religious seminarians (see Table 7). Seminarians may be choosing the diocesan priesthood more frequently because it is more in keeping with their theological beliefs, and they may feel more at home.

The number of seminarians for both diocesan and religious priesthood also continues to decline. The number of seminarians for the diocesan priesthood went from a high of 571 in 1987 to 406 in 1992, and an estimated 330 at the time of this study. Considering the overall decline in the number of seminarians for the priesthood, and in particular, for the religious priesthood, it can safely be assumed that the low numbers of religious seminarians must be having a devastating impact. Euart, writing on the transition of religious life toward the 21st century, observes:

> History shows that it is reasonable to expect that many, if not most religious communities in the church today will eventually go out of existence . . . . Revitalization calls for a transforming response to the signs and conditions of the times, a return to the spirit of the founder and a profound renewal of the life of prayer, faith and a centeredness on Christ.[3]

Two questions arise from this overall decline in vocations and religious vocations in particular. With the overall decline in the number of men studying for the priesthood, what will leadership in the Church of the future look like? How can the laity become involved in leading Church communities, and what authority will be vested in them? With the increasing number of priestly candidates from other places like Poland or Asia, what style of leadership can be anticipated from the Bishops, and experienced by the people?

Furthermore, what will be the impact of the decrease in numbers of religious priests in Canada? Religious were, at times, considered the teachers, missionaries and prophets in the Canadian Church. Many of these ministries have now been assumed by the laity. With declining numbers, can religious communities envision new directions for themselves? What is the face of the prophets and prophetic communities of tomorrow's Church?

---

[3] Euart 1994, 770.

Toward Regional Equality in the Distribution of Priests

Another trend is the continued regional decline in the number of priests/seminarians. This is true especially in Quebec and, somewhat less so, in the Atlantic Provinces. Table 5 (page 31) presents these results. Whereas in 1977, Quebec accounted for 42% of the diocesan priests in Canada, this had decreased to 35% in 1992. The research suggests that this decline has continued, since the Quebec diocesan seminarians made up only 32% of the study population. The province of Ontario seems to register the main increase in percentage of priests/seminarians over the past twenty–five years.

As the numbers of Church leaders shift regionally in Canada, from predominantly French–Canadian Catholic to a greater balance in the four regions of Canada, what shifts in power will take place, especially in the distribution of diocesan Bishops? For example, Asians are the largest group of seminarians born outside of Canada. Numerous European priests, and especially Polish ones, are now working in Canada. How will these groups be represented in places of power in the near future?

Toward More Homosexual Priests

A systematic study of the sexual orientation of seminarians has never been done prior to this study. There has been no way, therefore, to make comparisons over time or to trace trends. It is, however, "common wisdom" in seminary circles that the percentages of seminarians stating a homosexual orientation seems to be increasing. Murphy (1992) studied Catholic priests. Table 4 (page 30) suggests that over 25% of Catholic priests and seminarians state a sexual orientation other than heterosexual. The percentage of diocesan seminarians who profess a heterosexual orientation (74.3%) is virtually the same as the percentage of religious seminarians (74.1%). They differ in that a higher percentage of religious seminarians seem more certain of their homosexual orientation, while a greater percentage of diocesan seminarians state either that they are unsure or that they are bi–sexual in orientation.

Those seminarians who state that their sexual orientation is bi–sexual or that they are unsure also indicated more family dysfunctions, such as an alcoholic father or sexual abuse outside the family. From a developmental perspective, one would conclude that exposure to family dysfunctions can hinder the development of individuation and intimacy both in the family and, subsequently or simultaneously, with peers. It can have the effect of confusing individuals about their sexual identity, and also their identity as priests. How are these issues of family dysfunction resolved in the life of the seminarians, or addressed in seminary formation? With their admission of these family dysfunctions, one wonders about the effectiveness or impact of these seminarians in future ministry. These and other questions need to be addressed in further research.

Is homosexuality really out of the Church "closet," or is it thought that people really cannot tell who one is sexually, intimately or pastorally? What is the place of women in the lives of homosexually oriented Church ministers? These questions are addressed in Chapter 12, "Assessing Seminarians."

11

Recruitment of Seminarians

Recruitment for the priesthood is both an unstructured, inspirational process and a well–organized marketing plan. Insofar as it is a grace from God, it is beyond the limitations of this study. But inasmuch as recruitment is a marketing plan with a target population, a fairly specific "sales pitch," with funds committed to it, results of this study may assist in the task of recruiting priests.

Appealing to an Older Generation

One observation that arises immediately from the research is that the average age of seminarians continues to rise. Currently that average is 31.4 years old. Results indicate that older seminarians (that is, those more than 30 years of age) score significantly higher on the intergenerational triangulation scale, indicating that they are less triangulated with their parents. This further indicates a greater ability to maintain a sense of personal identity and individuation.

Current assumptions in the Church about the recruitment of "young men," be it high school recruitment or even college recruitment, should be reviewed. Indeed, a quick perusal of Butler's *Lives of the Saints* seems to indicate that many of these saints in the Church were older men and women when they began their ministry. This suggests that a more specific marketing plan for older men (30 years or more) should be conceived and implemented. Recruitment that is directed toward older, more professional men might mean money better spent.

Within seminarian formation itself, the change in average age suggests that a change in seminary formation is required. Whereas in 1966, 72% of seminarians were under the age of 25 years, today 42.3% of seminarians in Canada are over the age of 31 years. The composition of the seminary population is very different. The processes of seminarian formation will need to reflect this vastly different demographic reality.

For example, seminarians today should be offered an approach to learning that is more oriented to adults. Many of these men have lived on their own and some have held significant positions of employment before entering the seminary. Some have come from independent lifestyles and now face the prospect of joining a group that is essentially communal in nature. How are the individual's boundaries to be respected in this new setting? How will they adjust to a priestly life style that expects and practises obedience to authority? In fact, one might wonder if the decreased number of seminarians entering the religious priesthood might not reflect the preferences of older men for the more independent lifestyle of the diocesan priesthood.

Older seminarians have been in love, dated more often, and dated more steadily than their younger brothers in the seminary. Their scores on peer intimacy are significantly higher than younger seminarians. Furthermore, their experiences of intimacy would seem to be different. How is intimacy with peers to be lived in the seminary? How will celibacy be presented to them, and would this be different from the way it is presented to younger seminarians?

Williamson (1991) stated that the achievement of personal authority is begun in earnest in the fourth decade of life. Older seminarians might be engaged in this process in a more advanced manner than their younger counterparts. Does seminary formation foster or impede the achievement of personal authority? Future research using control groups might offer some insight here.

Previously Married Men

Responses to the survey questions indicated that seminarians who were previously married (four in total) were significantly less "triangulated" with parents. This is one indication of more personal authority. In his study of adult male maturity, Cebik (1988) found that intimacy and individuation in the spousal relationship, plus freedom to discuss personal matters with one's parents, are the best predictors of psychological development in males in the fourth and fifth decades of their lives. This leads us to the question: Because these previously married seminarians had spousal relationships, might they not have an advantage in terms of increased maturity and personal authority? Our research gathered no data regarding the nature of seminarians' previous marriage relationships. Nor did we examine the reasons for their terminations.

As the results appear to indicate more maturity for previously married seminarians, might this not open the door for more serious consideration of the ordination of married men? A married man was considered by Jesus to be worthy to become the first Pope. Married men were ordained to the priesthood in the Catholic Church for a thousand years. And with the declining numbers of seminarians for the priesthood, perhaps it is time to stop sacrificing the potential for increased personal authority and improved Church ministry on the altar of celibacy.

12

Assessing Seminarians

Seminarians for the priesthood go through a fairly extensive assessment procedure prior to their seminary formation, or at an early stage in it. This assessment usually takes the form of interviews and psychological testing. This section focuses on the implications of the results of this study for 1) the family–of–origin interview; 2) the sexual/social/intimacy interview; 3) the certainty of their decision for the priesthood; and 4) seminarian guardedness to being assessed.

A major goal of this study was to assess what factors and situations, especially within the seminarians' family of origin and experiences of intimacy, correlate with the varying degrees of personal authority. In the following discussion, I draw out the implications of the findings for the family–of–origin interview and the interview concerning sexual and social intimacy.

Family–of–Origin Interview

In the assessment process with potential seminarians, it has always been assumed that seminarians come from "good Catholic families," which term is defined, in part, as an intact family which practises the faith regularly. Results of this study indicate that families that practice their faith "strongly" scored significantly higher on intergenerational intimacy. In other words, it might be said that families that pray together seem to stay together. In the same way, seminarians who have not experienced separation, divorce or death of a parent are more able to be intimate with parents, and experience less intergenerational intimidation. Practice of faith in the family and experiences of separation, divorce or death become important questions to ask in any family–of–origin interview as part of the assessment process.[1]

Results suggest that in any assessment process, the family–of–origin interview should move beyond the notion of a "good Catholic family" and include as part of its focus possible family dysfunctions. Appendix B presents numerous family dysfunctions such as alcoholism, depression, and addiction in the father, mother or sibling. Results indicate that individuation and intimacy scores on the personal authority scale are lower when these dysfunctions are present. In other words, seminarians who have experienced these dysfunctions in their families would have more difficulty with individuation and intimacy with parents and peers, and they would be more intimidated by their parents and triangulated with them. Therefore, they would have less personal authority in their daily lives. It makes good sense, then, to take these dysfunctions in the family into account in any assessment of seminarians. These negative factors in the family–of–origin need to be seen as red flags for seminarian recruiters and alert those in charge of seminary formation to proceed with caution.

Further exploration of the seminarian and his family background is paramount. Family–of–origin counselling theories hold that one's current self–image, values, behaviours, attitudes and relations with others are regulated by one's family–of–origin experiences to varying degrees. Framo (1981) states that adults need to work through old family–of–origin issues in order to take the charge out of similar problems occurring in present–day situations and relationships.[2]

Greeley, reflecting on a 1969 survey of young priests in the United States, noted also that these priests tended to come from devout Catholic families.[3] In researching the relationship between "family tension" in one's past and resignation from the priesthood, Greeley found that

---

[1] Goldenberg and Goldenberg 1991, 147.

the hypothesis that a strain in family background will relate to resignation from the priesthood is supported by the studies. In every one of ten comparisons that can be made between resignees and actives, the resignees are more likely to report problems in the family background, and in some cases, the differences are quite substantial.[4]

The results of this study suggest that the occurrence of family violence and sexual abuse in the lives of seminarians today is lower than estimates of the national average for men. Seminarians who have experienced family violence and sexual abuse also scored lower on personal authority. They have less intimacy and individuation with parents and peers, and experience more intergenerational intimidation and triangulation. And although the numbers of seminarians who experienced sexual abuse in the family (N = 7) or outside the family (N = 16) are small in this study, the seminarians who stated that they were abusive to others (N = 2) also stated that they were first abused themselves. In light of the publicity of sexual abuse charges and convictions in the Church over the past few years, these family–of–origin issues must be taken very seriously. The 1992 report of the Canadian Conference of Catholic Bishop's Ad Hoc Committee on Sexual Abuse, "The Selection and the Formation of Candidates for the Priesthood," identified "vulnerability factors" that need to be assessed in the preliminary discernment

---

[2] Because Bowen believed that intergenerational patterns and influences are crucial determinants of present functioning, he developed a graphic way of representing the family of origin for assessment purposes. The family diagram or genogram is a pictorial form of an individual's family of origin, complete with names, sibling positions, marital status, occupations, religious affiliation, geographic locations, health issues, important dates, times, events, and relationship patterns such as voluntary closeness, enmeshment and cut–off, and the ebb and flow of family emotional processes. Individuation and intimacy patterns can also be delineated. McGoldrick and Gerson (1985), who have written extensively on genograms, suggest that family patterns tend to repeat themselves from one generation to the next unless unresolved issues are addressed.

[3] Greeley 1972a.
[4] Greeley 1972b, 32.

of candidates for the priesthood. Among these vulnerability factors are bodily identity, individual identity, psychosexual identity, psychosocial identity, and family environment. Under the heading of psychosexual identity are questions about sexual orientation, jealousy, sexual abuse and previous marriage.

Further research is needed in this area, but the results already give seminary recruiters many areas for deeper questioning and care. Although not predictive, the indicators surfacing in this research are nevertheless significant, and would lead those in positions of responsibility to determine whether there are "live" issues for a particular seminarian and if this person is able to handle these issues and grow.

Sexual/Social (Intimacy) Interview

The current study suggests that intimacy factors such as experiences of love or dating have a positive effect upon the seminarian's individuation and ability to be intimate, especially with his peers (see Appendix C). The results indicate that the seminarian's experiences of love, dating, steady dating, previous marriage, and length of friendships all contribute toward higher scores on personal authority. Seminarians who have experienced intimacy in these ways have more intimate relationships with their peers and achieve more personal authority. There was no indication that such experiences have any detrimental effect.

The results also indicate that sexual orientation can affect the achievement of personal authority. On the one hand, heterosexual seminarians scored higher on the intergenerational intimacy scale. On the other hand, seminarians who stated their sexual orientation as bisexual or unsure also experienced more dysfunction in their family of origin.

At the time of their ordination to the priesthood, seminarians make a promise of celibacy or the vow of chastity. Therefore, the way in which intimacy is experienced and lived becomes a crucial issue for their future. Murphy (1992) found that 62% of Catholic priests and religious brothers and sisters had engaged in sexual behaviour since the making of their promise or vow of celibacy. Murphy concludes that what does seem unique to vowed celibates in general is their conscious commitment to understanding and pursuing intimacy that is countercultural both to the prevailing male system and to their early training in religious and clerical life.[5]

Through a thorough sexual/social interview, those responsible for the assessment of seminarians are better able to determine the feasibility of the candidate for the celibate priestly life. Williamson defines personal authority in part as a pattern of abilities to "initiate or to receive intimacy voluntarily, in conjunction with the ability to set clear boundaries for the self at will."[6] As Murphy's study suggests, this balancing of intimacy and boundary–setting may be a tall order for any seminarian.

Certainty in the Desire To Become a Priest

One factor that is directly linked to the degree of personal authority is the measure of certainty on the part of the seminarians in regard to becoming priests. The more sure their decision, the higher the scores on many scales. Those seminarians who stated that they were "absolutely sure" indicated more individuation and intimacy with parents and peers, less triangulation and intimidation with parents, and higher scores on the personal authority scale. Although it is a rather simple question to ask, and its answer might be assumed, nevertheless it provides an abundance of information about the priest–to–be and can lead into an important area of conversation with potential seminarians.

Guardedness in the Assessment Process

In a workshop given at the Redemptorist Centre for Growth in Edmonton, one researcher stated that seminarians shared a high degree of defensiveness or guardedness on assessment

---

[5] Murphy 1992, 111.
[6] Bray and Williamson 1984, 168.

instruments like the MMPI–2.[7] Another who researched male and female Protestant candidates for clergy found that

> the need by these future ministers for social approval and their corresponding desire to avoid rejection and conflict suggest that they may have a difficult time taking risks that would endanger their "approval rating."[8]

Guardedness in seminarians, especially during the assessment process and in the first years of seminary formation, seems to be the expected modus operandi. After all, seminarians are seeking approval of their desire to become priests. Moreover, it is a process of evaluation: naturally, they put their best foot forward. It is well known that some of their colleagues are asked to leave. How much they trust the assessment and formation process is an open question. How much they trust the "will of God" in calling them to priesthood is a genuine question, too.

Guardedness can be greatly reduced through intensive interviews on the family–of–origin and sexual/social intimacy. These interviews are more than just a means of assessment. They also encourage further self–understanding and further growth. These interviews take place over an extended period, and encourage dialogue between the seminarians and the professionals who conduct them. Furthermore, the seminarians can learn about themselves objectively through instruments such as the genogram or the MMPI–2, and can be encouraged to continue to pursue personal growth through the years of seminary formation.

Family–of–origin theory suggests that an individual acquires from early family experiences a set of explicit and implicit expectations, attitudes and beliefs which serve as personal points of reference for the living out of all interpersonal life. Further understanding of these family expectations will allow the seminarian to

---

[7] Douziech 1994. The Minnesota Multiphasic Personality Inventory (MMPI–2) is currently the most widely used and researched objective instrument for personality inventory. Among the numerous scales are three which measure the validity of the responses, including a scale for "guardedness."

[8] Sullender 1993, 272.

discard those expectations that might be seen as unhealthy, and to connect intimately with family and peers in a new way.

The assessment process also permits the seminarian to discern further the will of God. Openness to God, to spiritual direction and to the staff of the seminary are aspects of this discernment. Guardedness suggests that the seminarian might not be as open to the possibility of not being called to the priesthood.

This question of guardedness is closely connected to personal authority. As Williamson defines it, personal authority is, in part, the ability to order and direct one's own thoughts and opinions, to choose to express or withhold one's thoughts and opinions regardless of social pressure, and to take responsibility for the totality of one's life.

Seminarian Formation

Once given the green light in the assessment process, a seminarian begins to be moulded in a Catholic seminary or house of formation. Those involved in seminarian formation may need to consider the following issues that arise from the findings of this study: 1) the significance of ethnic background; and 2) changes in personal authority and in theological attitudes over the years that seminarians are in the seminary.

Ethnic Differences

Ethnic factors were found to be statistically significant on five of the scales measuring personal authority and on the scale measuring theological attitude. Appendix E presents these results.

Of note is the fact that those seminarians who identified their ethnic background as Asian scored lowest in the areas of intergenerational individuation and personal authority. It would seem that their relationships to their families and peers may be quite different from that of other seminarians. They tend to have less ability to individuate from parents and to make independent decisions. They also have less personal authority in their relationships with parents.

French Canadian seminarians scored lowest on peer individuation, indicating less ability to make decisions independently of peers. These results are in keeping with some ethnic differences found by Krikorian (1990).[9] The results of the current study raise questions about the various ways that ethnic groups live out the interplay between individuation and intimacy in their own families and with peers. The lower scoring of Asian seminarians in particular raises questions about the ability of the Personal Authority in the Family System Questionnaire – College Version to operationalize a definition of personal authority that can truly respect different ethnicities and cultures.

Is personal authority, defined as the synthesizing of individuation and intimacy, an appropriate way of describing maturity of life and readiness for responsibilities such as the priesthood? Is the notion of personal authority a North American, white–Anglo–Saxon concept that is inappropriate to people of other cultures and ethnic backgrounds? To answer these questions, one might want to look at seminary life itself, and consider the relationships of seminarians from different ethnic backgrounds to each other, and to those who conduct the formation program. How are intimacy and individuation lived out concretely? How will seminarians from different cultures be assessed? The results of this study suggest that sensitivity to other ethnic groups is a real issue in seminarian formation. Further study is needed in order to investigate fully the implications of ethnic differences in the life of Catholic seminarians in Canada today. And then there is the practical question: How would seminarians from different backgrounds be encouraged to develop in the areas of individuation and intimacy while in the seminary formation program?

Theological Year

Do seminarians have different degrees of personal authority and different theological attitudes depending on their years of study? Are there trends and changes that might be attributed to changes over time spent in the seminary? Put another way: What

---

[9] Caperton–Brown (1992) also found ethnic as well as gender differences on PAFS–QVC scales.

effect might seminary formation itself have upon the issues of individuation and intimacy in the lives of Catholic seminarians?

Peer intimacy scores tend to rise slowly over the six years that most seminarians are in theology and in seminary formation (see Appendix D). This may indicate an increased capacity for intimacy. This may be due in part to increased age, which has also been shown to increase scores on the PAFS–QVC scale. It may also be the result of direct interventions during the formative years of seminary training. Indeed, an increasing number of seminaries are addressing the issue of social–sexual development in their formation programs.

Peer individuation scores also tend to rise slightly over the years, except for a significant drop during the pastoral year. The pastoral year is one or two years spent outside the seminary in a pastoral or ministry setting. Although usually they work with an older priest, in many ways seminarians are "on their own." Lower peer individuation scores reflect less ability to act in an autonomous or differentiated manner. This is usually their first experience of ministry on a full–time basis. They are called upon to become public persons and to lead people in the practice of religion. Perhaps it is the insertion into the larger world that diminishes their ability to act as individuals. In a similar vein, personal authority also takes a dip in the third year of theology, which for some seminarians is their pastoral experience or the year just prior to their pastoral year. Anticipating the pastoral experience may be enough to shake their confidence.

Theological attitude scores tend to shift toward a more modern theological attitude over the first years of theology until the pastoral year. During the last two years, including the pastoral year, their theological attitude becomes more traditional. Nonetheless, they are still more modern in their theological attitudes when they leave the seminary than when they began. Their main focus is the study of theology as a discipline of pastoral work, but the seminary is also an agent of socialization which helps to turn the seminarian into a priest. It is reasonable to assume that both these facets of seminary life contribute to making them more modern in their theological thinking than when they arrived.

Personal Authority over the Years

After approximately six years in seminary formation, the seminarian is ordained a priest and he is sent to minister, primarily in parish settings. Can this study help us foresee future changes in the character of seminarians? What changes in personal authority scores can we expect to see over the years in the seminary?

From the results of this study, it is noted that maturity or personal authority tends to increase steadily and surely. There are dips and high points in the statistics, but the general pattern is toward increased scores. This change is especially apparent in the areas of intergenerational intimidation and intergenerational triangulation. As they grow older, seminarians indicate that they feel less intimidated or triangulated by their parents. Williamson states that

> the most difficult problem for son or daughter is intergenerational intimidation. Intergenerational intimidation in its myriad forms is unquestionably the major obstacle in the way of the renegotiation of family politics and the establishment of personal authority in the family and therefore life.[10]

At the heart of intergenerational intimidation, he suggests, is the unconscious fear that calling into question the established social and political order, including the uses of power in the family of origin, may bring about such evils as one's own death or the death of one's parent(s).

Decreased intimidation in the lives of seminarians during their years of formation augurs well for increased achievement of personal authority in their lives. And indeed, scores on the personal authority scale also tend to increase over the years.

The one notable dip in many scores measuring personal authority is that for seminarians in their pastoral year. Pastoral year seminarians score on the low side of all four intergenerational scales, which indicates that for this period they are less

---

[10] Williamson 1991, 8.

intimate with their parents, less "their own persons," more intimidated by parents, and more involved in a family triangle. Perhaps one reason for this decreased score is that many seminarians go "back home" for their pastoral experience, or return to within travelling distance of their home. In other words, they return to a family which they probably left three or four years earlier – to a family system that, most likely, has not changed much.[11] The dip in scores is not great: they return only to the level of first–year seminarians, who may be considered to have just left home.[12]

As Appendix D suggests, once back in the seminary (theology years four and five) most personal authority scores jump to a higher level than those of the pre–pastoral year. One might wonder, therefore, if life in the seminary might not be too isolated from the real world, leading to the development of what Kerr and Bowen call a "pseudo–self." They describe the pseudo–self as

> knowledge and beliefs acquired from others that are incorporated by the intellect and [are] negotiable in relationships with others . . . . [T]he principles and beliefs of [the] pseudo–self are quickly changed to enhance one's image with others or to oppose others . . . . [The] pseudo–self is a "pretend" self . . . . [T]he higher level of functioning is totally dependent on the group's continued support.[13]

In contrast, the "solid self" is composed of firmly held convictions and beliefs which are established slowly and can be changed only from within the self. One needs to ask, however, if this return to a former self in the pastoral year also suggests a similar return once the seminarian has completed formation and begins working in a parish back home? What will he be like then?

---

[11] This is suggested by Bowen (1978).
[12] This pattern conforms with Bowen's (1978) contention that family systems do not change much over short periods of time, and that emotional processes within a family are always there unless serious efforts are made by the seminarian to distance himself from them.
[13] Kerr and Bowen 1988, 104–105.

The Seminarians' Relationships to Women

A second issue that needs to be addressed is that of the place of women in the lives of Catholic seminarians. Both younger and older seminarians stated that they can feel most intimate with Jesus/God or another man, but that they seem to have more difficulty feeling intimate with a woman. When sexual orientation is considered, a larger proportion of heterosexual seminarians stated that they feel most intimate with Jesus or God, followed by those who feel most intimate with women, and then those who feel most intimate with other men. The largest proportion of homosexual seminarians stated that they feel most intimate with other men, followed by those who feel most intimate with Jesus or God, and finally (a distant third) those who feel most intimate with women. One naturally asks: How will these priests–to–be interact with women who make up the majority of parish communities? Would women also take a lower place in the attention and ministry of these seminarians? In an age when Catholic women are striving to take their rightful place, or, for that matter, any place, they will have to interact more and more with these future Church leaders who are now in the seminary. How successful will these seminarians be in remaining individuated or autonomous while simultaneously and voluntarily remaining connected and open to women as their "peers in the experience of being human"?[14]

Gilligan (1982) argues that most present–day psychological theories are male–oriented and that women see development differently. She writes, "There seems to be a line of development missing from current depictions of adult development, a failure to describe the progression of relationships toward a maturity of interdependence."[15]

Gilligan argues that individuation in relation to peers (which she terms identity) and peer intimacy are one and the same process for women. Will Catholic seminarians in Canada today be able to balance these two forces in their relationship with

---

[14] Bray and Williamson 1984, 168.
[15] Gilligan 1982, 155.

women to the same degree that they do with men? Where are the qualities of equality and mutuality both in interpersonal relationships with women and in ministry with women? How will these priests–to–be minister to the women of their parishes or deal with female spiritual growth?

The current study indicates that seminarians feel more intimate with their mothers than with their fathers.[16] However, this intergenerational intimacy may have a very different dynamic than intimacy with peers, even if Williamson suggests that the ultimate work of personal authority is to relate to *all* other persons, including "former parents," as peers.

Throughout the literature on priests there is frequent reference to the "mother influence." Potvin and Suziedelis (1969) wrote that the mother is more likely to be the more influential parent in the development of a priestly vocation. Greeley (1972a) found that encouragement for vocation is twice as likely to come from the mother than the father (30% compared to 16%). And Godin (1983) commented that the mother is always more favourably disposed toward the vocation of her son than is the father.

Still, the difference in intergenerational intimidation between mothers and fathers is minimal: seminarians said they felt only slightly more intimidated by fathers than by mothers.[17] So if mothers are a significant influence, it appears that this influence is felt through encouragement and love rather than through any form of intimidation. This raises more questions: How does the seminarians' intimacy with women compare to their intimacy with their mothers? Is their intimacy with other women son–to–mother–like?

---

[16] The mean score for the relationship with mothers on the intergenerational intimacy scale was 41.6; the mean score for relationships with fathers was 37.9.

[17] The mean intergenerational intimidation scale scores computed according to mother and father were 18.2 and 18.1 respectively.

13

Conclusions, Questions and Recommendations

This study contributes to our knowledge of Roman Catholic seminarians in Canada, and particularly to our understanding of the influences of the family and experiences of intimacy upon their achievement of personal authority. On the basis of the quantitative data presented here and information gathered from related case studies,[18] several conclusions can be presented.

1) Seminarians have greater personal authority and maturity than the normative group of men, and roughly the same degree as that found among other groups. Roman Catholic seminarians in Canada are neither remarkably mature nor immature. The good news is that the widespread criticism of unhealthy seminarians and priests is not proved true. On the other hand, there is still much to be done in seminary formation to develop priests who will become not merely like "ordinary folks," but the next leaders of Church and society. Given the greater frequency of intact families of origin and of the regular practice of family faith, and given the lesser frequency of family dysfunctions, family violence and sexual abuse, one would expect to see more maturity. Ques-

---

[18] Rovers 1995. In my doctoral dissertation I interviewed ten seminarians with various family-of-origin, intimacy and PAFS-QVC scores. Three of these interviews were written up.

tions persist about the lived expression of intimacy and celibacy in the lives of seminarians and priests.
2) A vast array of issues, especially concerning the family of origin and the seminarians' experiences of intimacy, needs to be addressed in the process of assessing candidates for the priesthood. Questions about these matters should be incorporated into an expanded family–of–origin interview and a sexual/social interview, and trained assessment personnel and Church leaders must be willing to use this information in the process of assessment prior to a candidate's entry into theology.

What should be the criteria for acceptance or rejection of a candidate, especially in light of the changing profile of seminarians and their dwindling numbers? Our research has correlated numerous family–of–origin and intimacy factors with healthier scores on the Personal Authority in the Family System Questionnaire. These include: age of seminarians; ethnic background; practice of family faith; marriage status of parents; parental or sibling dysfunctions such as alcohol abuse or depression; experience of family violence and sexual abuse; sexual orientation; various experiences of being in love and dating; friendships and the ability to be intimate with others; and decisiveness about becoming a priest. It would seem vital that these and other family–of–origin and intimacy factors form the nucleus of the criteria for admission today to the priesthood.

3) Considering the complexity of the lives of seminarians today, and the changing face of seminary formation, those who conduct the formation of seminarians must acquire skills in psychological and human development. In a Church that has always stressed the spiritual aspects of seminary formation, these new psychological realities should be incorporated somehow into the spiritual aspects.

4) Though counselling has been seen in the past as an exception to the norm, it appears to be much more important today in determining which candidates ought to remain in the seminary, and to be vital in helping seminarians grow in personal authority. Overall, seminarians respond affirmatively to counselling. The questions remain: When should one insist

that a potential candidate receive counselling, and is this best done prior to entry into the seminary?
5) The issue of the seminarians' ministry and relationship to women should be addressed directly. Women now form a majority in the Church, and we see, generally speaking, that seminarians are less inclined to connect equitably with women. Might the inclusion of women in the formation staff be part of the solution? Would the ordination or appointment of women to minister more specifically to other women also help here?
6) The Church should come to grips with the fact that the theological attitudes of future priests are becoming more traditional, and consider the possible implications for ministry in a Church which may be broader in theological attitude than its priesthood.
7) As the Church in general, and seminarians in particular, become more ethnically diverse, cultural differences need to be taken into consideration in the process of seminary formation. This is especially true for Asian seminarians, but it is also true for English–speaking and French–speaking Canadian seminarians.

Implications for Future Research

Our study is only a first step. Further research needs to be done in specific areas and in greater detail. Research on the variables of the family of origin and of intimacy and sexuality might yield more detailed findings. In particular, the current findings on theological attitudes call for a new approach to measuring theological attitudes.

It would be interesting and worthwhile to conduct a longitudinal study of seminarians using the Personal Authority in the Family System Questionnaire – College Version, and family–of–origin and sexual/social interviews, with some of the class as a control group. If seminary personnel were to deal directly with family–of–origin and intimacy factors during seminary formation, would this increase personal authority measurably over the five or six years of seminary formation? Would the questionnaire have predictive value, so that it could be used more decisively in assessing candidates?

Many variables, especially those in the family of origin and experiences of intimacy, are currently receiving heightened attention in the process of formation. I hope that this study will enhance our awareness of the numerous variables that influence the lives of seminarians in Canada today. May this improved understanding also contribute to even greater maturity or personal authority in the future leaders of the Church.

Appendix A
The Questionnaire to Seminarians

Differentiation of Self in Roman Catholic Seminarians in Canada: A National Survey Questionnaire

Dear Seminarian/Scholastic:

This Canada–wide survey is being conducted to gather information from students preparing for the priesthood. Your input will be of great value to vocations ministry, seminary formation and the future of the priesthood.

I am in seminary formation myself and I am doing a doctoral study at the University of Alberta. The main aspect of this study is to examine the influence of the family of origin upon one's present functioning.

YOUR ANSWERS ARE STRICTLY ANONYMOUS. No one at the seminary will, at any time, have access to this questionnaire. No identification information will be collected. We therefore encourage you to be completely honest, as this will give the most accurate results.

You have the right not to fill out this questionnaire. Please be aware that by filling out this questionnaire you are consenting to have your responses used in a research project. Or you may fill out this questionnaire and not answer specific questions.

I suggest that you set aside about 40 minutes to do this questionnaire in the next week. Please answer the questions as accurately as possible in their given order. Since your questions express your personal and honest experience, please do not discuss this questionnaire with other seminarians until all are completed.

I would like to conduct several one–hour interviews based upon this questionnaire. These interviews will take place after

Christmas. If you are open to be interviewed, please sign your name and phone number on the front page of the questionnaire.

If you do not wish to be interviewed, please leave the questionnaire unsigned to ensure your anonymity.

When you have finished, insert the questionnaire into the enclosed envelope and return it in the mail. Thank you for your honesty and cooperation.

Sincerely,
Martin Rovers, O.M.I.

The following questions are to gather personal information about seminarians in Canada. Please circle the number opposite your response.

[Note: The questionnaire as it is presented here contains the data which was obtained.]

101 Are you destined for one of the following?

Diocesan priesthood 72.8%
Religious priesthood, society or community 26.7%
Other (Specify) 0.5%

102 What was your age on your last birthday?

Years Old 31.4 years

103 In what year of theology are you now enrolled?

First 24.9%
Second 20.9%
Third 19.9%
Fourth 6.5%
Fifth 10.0%
Pastoral year 17.9%

104 What part of Canada are you affiliated with in terms of diocese or religious community?

Atlantic provinces 13.9%
Quebec 35.6%
Ontario 34.7%
Western provinces 15.8%
Yukon and the Territories .... —

105 Where were you born?

In Canada 86.2%
Europe 4.4%
Asia 5.4%
Africa 0.5%
South or Central America .... —
USA 3.0%
Australia / New Zealand .... —

106 Which racial or national background best describes your family?

_____

107 What is your Myers–Briggs personality type? _____

Using the responses below, how frequently have you engaged in the following activities BEFORE entering the seminary or theology. *(Write one number on each line.)*

RESPONSES:
1. NEVER INVOLVED
2. INVOLVED ONCE OR TWICE
3. INVOLVED ON AN IRREGULAR BASIS
4. INVOLVED ON A REGULAR BASIS

	Percentage Involved on a Regular Basis
201 Charismatic group	14%
202 Cursillo	7%
203 Teaching religion	17%
204 Lay volunteer	41%
205 A member of a parish council	10%
206 Eucharistic minister or lector in parish	40%
207 Being a boy scout	25%
208 Being an altar boy	47%
209 Working in a rectory or religious community	19%
210 Engaged in social work	17%
211 Engaged in hospital work	8%
212 Engaged in community work	21%
213 Being a teacher in a Catholic school	6%
214 Being a teacher in a public school	5%

215 SEARCH, TEC, IMPACT, CHALLENGE,
COR, and encounter program 7%
216 Vocational discernment weekends or associate
programs 10%
217 Other – *Please specify*... ___

The following questions are meant to obtain demographics on your family of origin (the family you grew up in or with whom you spent most of your childhood days).

301 How many children were ever born to your father and mother?

                                        Number of Children   4.8

302 In your family of origin, are you

    an only child 3.0%
    the oldest child 27.9%
    a middle child 46.3%
    the youngest child 22.9%

303 What was the religious affiliation of your parents?

    Mother Catholic, Father Catholic 89.7%
    Mother Catholic, Father other 3.9%
    Mother other, Father Catholic 2.5%
    Mother other, Father other 3.9%

304 How was faith practised in your family?

    strongly (Sunday mass, prayer, talk faith) 38.1%
    moderately (Sunday mass, occasional prayer) 49.5%
    somewhat (occasional mass, no prayer) 2.5%
    little (Christmas/Easter mass, no prayer) 7.9%
    not at all 2.0%

305 How was faith practised by you after you left home?

strongly 57.6%
moderately 28.1%
somewhat 4.9%
little 4.9%
not at all 4.4%

306 Which of these general groups best fits your estimate of your family's annual income at the present time?

less than 20,000 .... 27.2%
20,000 – 39,999 .... 34.3%
40,000 – 59,999 .... 22.6%
60,000 – 79,999 .... 9.7%
above 80,000 .... 6.2%

307 What is the most recent marital status of your parents?

married once 68.7%
separated/divorced 7.0%
widowed 19.4%
remarried 4.5%
never married 0.5%

308 If your parents were separated, divorced or widowed, how old were you at the time of the first incident?

Years Old 18.5

309 Do any of the following apply to your father?
(*circle* as many as applicable)

	YES	NO
alcoholic	23.6	76.4
general depression or anxiety	11.6	88.4
drug addiction	2.5	97.5
other dysfunction (Specify)_____	7.1	92.9

310 Do any of the following apply to your mother?
(*circle* as many as applicable)

	YES	NO
alcoholic	2.0	98.0
general depression or anxiety	15.6	84.4

drug addiction	−	100.0
other dysfunction (Specify)_____	... 3.5	96.5

311 Do any of the following apply to any brother or sister. (*circle* as many as applicable)

	YES	NO
alcoholic	14.1	85.9
general depression or anxiety	14.7	85.3
drug addiction	7.6	92.4
other dysfunction (Specify)_____	8.1	91.9

312 While growing up in your family of origin, did you experience family violence? (emotional or physical violence between parents or between parents and children, or among children)

	YES	NO
family violence		
If your response is YES	30.8	69.2
I witnessed violence	25.9	74.1
I was a victim of violence	19.4	80.6.
I was violent to others in my family	8.4	91.6

313 While growing up, did you experience sexual abuse by someone IN your family? (inappropriately exposed or subjected to sexual contact, activity or behaviour)

	YES	NO
sexual abuse		
If your answer is YES	3.4	96.6
I witnessed abuse	0.5	99.5
I was a victim of sexual abuse	3.0	97.0
I was abusive to other family members	0.5	99.5

314 While growing up, were you sexually abused by someone *outside* your family?

	YES	NO
sexual abuse		
If your answer is YES	8.0	92.0
I witnessed abuse	1.5	98.5
I was a victim of sexual abuse	8.0	92.0
I was abusive to people outside my family	1.0	99.0

315 How old were you when you left home? (first moved out of your parents' house into another living accommodation)

                                                                 Years Old 19.7

316 Why did you leave home? (*circle* one only)

    to go to the seminary 29.2%
    to go to university 38.1%
    to go to work 17.3%
    to get out of the house 12.4%
    other (Specify)_____ 3.0%

317 In how many different living accommodations did you live between leaving home and entering the seminary or religious community?

                                               (circle one only)
    none (from home to seminary/community)........... 24.5%
    1–2 .... 28.5%
    3–5 .... 24.5%
    6+.. 22.5%

Please indicate true or false.

	TRUE	FALSE
350 Compared to others, our family is very close	73.9	26.1
351 I do not think my parents are (were) as compatible as most	30.2	69.8
352 My parents do not (did not) talk to each other enough	36.5	63.5
353 My parents really love (loved) each other	80.7	19.3
354 There are things I would like to change about my family	63.1	36.9
355 I was not happy at home	21.3	78.7
356 My parents disagreed on many things	29.9	70.1
357 My parents often quarrelled at home	26.8	73.2

The following questions are to observe dating patterns prior to theology as well as to gauge attitudes toward celibacy.

401 What is your sexual orientation now?

heterosexual 74.5%
homosexual 12.5%
bi-sexual 6.5%
unsure 6.5%

402 Have you ever been in love?

Yes 88.5%
No 11.5%

403 Did you ever date before coming into theology?

Yes 82.7%
No 17.3%

404 Did you date one person steadily (more than three months) before coming into theology?

Yes 68.7%
No 31.3%

405 Have you seriously considered the option of marriage?

Yes 64.2%
No 35.8%

406 Have you ever been married?

Yes 3.0%
No 97.0%

407 My best friend is

a man 50.5%
a woman 16.5%
Jesus/God 25.0%
other (Specify) _____ 8.0%

408 My best friend has been my best friend for
Number of years 10.8%

409 I feel I can be most intimate with
- a man 27.3%
- a woman 23.7%
- Jesus/God 34.3%
- other (specify) _____ 14.6%

410 I feel most intimate with (circle one only)
- a fellow seminarian 19.8%
- a friend outside the seminary/community 39.6%
- a brother/sister in my family 5.6%
- mom or dad 4.1%
- Jesus/God 31.0%

411 At what age did you know you wanted to be a priest?
- Age 20.4

412 What SINGLE factor was the greatest influence on your decision to become a priest? (Please choose ONLY one)
- a priest's example 15.3%
- an inner call 46.5%
- close involvement with church ministry 7.9%
- a retreat or time of discernment 7.4%
- the influence of parents or a relative 3.0%
- a religious brother or sister 2.0%
- a desire to help others 16.3%
- other (specify)_____ 1.5%

413 How decisive are you about your decision to become a priest?
- absolutely sure 28.9%
- sure 53.7%
- unsure 15.9%
- very unsure 1.5%

414 Do you think all diocesan priests should be required to make a promise of celibacy?
- yes, a perpetual promise 56.9%
- yes, a temporary promise 7.9%
- no, none at all 20.3%
- I don't know 14.9%

415 Do you think all religious priests should be required to take a vow of celibacy?

yes, a perpetual vow 75.5%
yes, a temporary vow 5.5%
no, none at all... 7.5%
I don't know.. 11.5%

416 If the church were to permit it, would you, as a priest, seriously consider marrying?

definitely would... 5.4%
probably would 12.4%
don't know 18.3%
probably not 43.1%
definitely not 20.8%

The following statements are designed to measure your theological attitudes. Please use the following scale to indicate the degree of your agreement or disagreement with the following statements.

1	2	3	4	5
Strongly Agree	Agree Somewhat	Uncertain	Disagree Somewhat	Strongly Disagree

85. Today's Christian must emphasize more than ever openness to the spirit rather than dependence upon traditional ecclesiastical structures.
    1 2 3 4 5

86. I think of God primarily as the Supreme Being, immutable, all powerful and the Creator of the universe.
    1 2 3 4 5

87. Salvation is mainly liberation from sin. It has to do with the well–being of souls and their preparation for eternal life.
1   2   3   4   5

88. I think of Jesus Christ as the God who humbled himself by becoming man and dying for my sins.
1   2   3   4   5

89. For me, God is found principally in my relationship with people.
1   2   3   4   5

90. Salvation is total liberation from both individual and collective sin, from injustice and inhuman conditions in the here and now.
1   2   3   4   5

91. Faith is primarily an encounter with God in Jesus Christ, rather than an assent to a coherent set of defined truths.
1   2   3   4   5

92. The primary task of the Church is to encourage its members to live the christian life, rather than to try to reform the world.
1   2   3   4   5

93. There are times when a person has to obey his or her personal conscience rather than the Church's teaching.
1   2   3   4   5

94. When I experience moments of deep communication and union with other persons, these sometimes strike me as a taste of what heaven would be like.
1   2   3   4   5

95. A Christian should primarily be concerned with the salvation of his or her own soul; then he or she should be concerned about helping others.
1   2   3   4   5

96. The important thing to stress when teaching about Jesus is that he is truly God, and therefore adoration should be directed toward Him.

       1   2   3   4   5

Thank you for your support. Please place in envelope and return AS SOON AS POSSIBLE.

Appendix B
Family-of-Origin Statistics

(Significant Mean Differences
on the Personal Authority in the Family System Questionnaire (College Version)
and on Theological Attitude Scale Scores and Family–of–Origin Factors)

Factor	Intergenerational Intimacy	Intergenerational Individuation	Intergenerational Intimidation	Intergenerational Triangulation	Peer Intimacy	Peer Individuation	Personal Authority	Theological Attitude
Group Mean Scores	90.4	32.4	35.9	32.2	46.5	32.7	45.5	37.2
Practice of Family Faith								
Strongly (N=66)	96.0							
Moderately (N=91)	88.9							
Somewhat (N=4)	75.0							
Little (N=15)	76.9							
Not at all (N=3)	96.3							
F-ratio	6.312*							

Note: * $p < .01$; ** $p < .05$

APPENDIX B

Factor	Intergenerational Intimacy	Intergenerational Individuation	Intergenerational Intimidation	Intergenerational Triangulation	Peer Intimacy	Peer Individuation	Personal Authority	Theological Attitude
Marital Status								
Marry Once (N=131)	94.0		36.5					
Widowed (N=14)	78.2		33.7					
Separated or Divorced (N=28)	79.8		36.7					
Remarried (N=6)	92.7		33.7					
Never Married (N=1)	79.0		25.0					
F-ratio	8.294*		3.343*					
Group Mean Scores	90.4	32.4	35.9	32.2	46.5	32.7	45.5	37.2
Father Alcoholic								
Yes (N=42)	80.8	30.7		30.6				
No (N=135)	93.1	33.0		32.8				
F-ratio	19.91*	5.66**		5.62**				

Note: * p < .01; ** p < .05.

Factor	Intergenerational Intimacy	Intergenerational Individuation	Intergenerational Intimidation	Intergenerational Triangulation	Peer Intimacy	Peer Individuation	Personal Authority	Theological Attitude
			Father Depressed					
Yes (N=23)	81.9	30.4		30.0				
No (N=153)	92.0	32.9		32.8				
F-ratio	9.60*	5.48**		6.95*				
			Father Addicted					
Yes (N=5)	62.2	23.4	24.8	22.2				
No (N=172)	91.0	32.7	36.2	32.5				
F-ratio	16.18*	15.46*	26.93*	19.77*				
			Father Dysfunctional					
Yes (N=13)		29.6					41.0	
No (N=163)		32.8					46.1	
F-ratio		5.51**					4.04**	

Note: * p < .01; ** p < .05.

APPENDIX B

Factor	Intergenerational Intimacy	Intergenerational Individuation	Intergenerational Intimidation	Intergenerational Triangulation	Peer Intimacy	Peer Individuation	Personal Authority	Theological Attitude
Mother Alcoholic								
Yes (N=4)		27.0						
No (N=172)		32.7						
F-ratio		6.64**						
Mother Depressed								
Yes (N=29)	82.3	29.2		29.7				
No (N=148)	91.7	33.0		32.7				
F-ratio	8.20*	13.11**		7.50*				
Group Mean Scores	90.4	32.4	35.9	32.2	46.5	32.7	45.5	37.2
Mother Dysfunctional								
Yes (N=7)	74.4				40.1		36.3.	
No (N=169)	91.4				46.7		46.1	
F-ratio	8.95*				9.47*		8.53*	

Note: * $p < .01$; ** $p < .05$.

Factor	Intergenerational Intimacy	Intergenerational Individuation	Intergenerational Intimidation	Intergenerational Triangulation	Peer Intimacy	Peer Individuation	Personal Authority	Theological Attitude
Sibling Alcoholic								
Yes (N=26)	82.1							
No (N=151)	91.6							
F-ratio	7.69*							
Sibling Addicted								
Yes (N=14)	79.2			28.6				40.6
No (N=163)	91.1			32.6				36.9
F-ratio	6.99*			7.06*				3.80**
Family Violence								
Yes (N=54)	81.7	29.4	34.6	29.4				
No (N=124)	94.3	33.8	36.5	33.6				
F-ratio	25.30*	27.22*	5.37**	25.25*				

Note: * $p < .01$; ** $p < .05$.

APPENDIX B

Factor	Intergenerational Intimacy	Intergenerational Individuation	Intergenerational Intimidation	Intergenerational Triangulation	Peer Intimacy	Peer Individuation	Personal Authority	Theological Attitude
			Witness Family Violence					
Yes (N=46)	83.5	29.7		29.8				
No (N=132)	92.9	33.4		33.1				
F-ratio	12.06*	18.02*		14.90*				
			Victim of Family Violence					
Yes (N=33)	76.2	28.7	34.4	30.0				
No (N=145)	93.7	33.3	36.3	32.8				
F-ratio	36.60*	21.97*	3.76**	8.01*				
			Sexually Abused Inside the Family					
Yes (N=16)					50.1			
No (N=177)					46.2			
F-ratio					7.18*			

Note: * p < .01; ** p < .05.

Factor	Intergenerational Intimacy	Intergenerational Individuation	Intergenerational Intimidation	Intergenerational Triangulation	Peer Intimacy	Peer Individuation	Personal Authority	Theological Attitude
		Victim of Sexual Abuse Outside the Family						
Yes (N=14)					50.0			
No (N=164)					46.2			
F–ratio					7.18*			

Note: * $p < .01$; ** $p < .05$.

Appendix C
Intimacy Statistics

(Significant Mean Differences on PAFS–QVC and Theological Attitude Scale Scores and Intimacy Factors)

Factor	Intergenerational Intimacy	Intergenerational Individuation	Intergenerational Intimidation	Intergenerational Triangulation	Peer Intimacy	Peer Individuation	Personal Authority	Theological Attitude
Group Mean Scores	90.4	32.4	35.9	32.2	46.5	32.7	45.5	37.2
Sexual Orientation								
Heterosexual (N=132)	92.4							36.3
Homosexual (N=24)	86.4							41.0
Bisexual (N=10)	81.5							35.9
Unsure (N=12)	83.4							40.8
F-ratio	2.95**							5.49**

Note: * p < .01; ** p < .05.

APPENDIX C

Factor	Intergenerational Intimacy	Intergenerational Individuation	Intergenerational Intimidation	Intergenerational Triangulation	Peer Intimacy	Peer Individuation	Personal Authority	Theological Attitude
Been In Love								
Yes (N=157)					46.8		46.0	
No (N=21)					43.7		41.3	
F-ratio					5.81**		4.50**	
Dated Prior to Theology								
Yes (N=146)						33.1	46.3	
No (N=34)						30.9	42.3	
F-ratio						5.33**	5.43**	
Dated Steadily Three Months Prior to Theology								
Yes (N=120)					47.1	33.3	47.2	
No (N=59)					45.3	31.3	42.0	
F-ratio					4.23**	6.93*	14.08*	

Note: * $p < .01$; ** $p < .05$.

Factor	Intergenerational Intimacy	Intergenerational Individuation	Intergenerational Intimidation	Intergenerational Triangulation	Peer Intimacy	Peer Individuation	Personal Authority	Theological Attitude
Considered Marriage Prior to Theology								
Yes (N=113)				31.7			46.5	36.3
No (N=66)				33.3			43.9	38.7
F-ratio				4.03**			3.75**	6.50*
Been Married Prior to Theology								
Yes (N=4)				39.2				
No (N=176)				32.1				
F-ratio				8.89*				
My Best Friend Is:								
A Man (N=91)				33.0				37.6
A Woman (N=31)				29.1				39.3
Jesus or God (N=44)				32.8				34.1
Other (N=14)				32.1				39.4
F-ratio				4.60*				6.35*

Note: * $p < .01$; ** $p < .05$.

APPENDIX C

Factor	Intergenerational Intimacy	Intergenerational Individuation	Intergenerational Intimidation	Intergenerational Triangulation	Peer Intimacy	Peer Individuation	Personal Authority	Theological Attitude
			How Long My Best Friend					
1-3 years (N=29)	82.9	29.5		29.9				
4-6 years (N=38)	87.9	33.5		33.0				
7-10 years (N=39)	93.1	32.9		30.7				
11-20 years (N=44)	93.3	33.0		33.3				
21 + years (N=15)	100.6	34.6		35.4				
F-ratio	4.33*	3.43*		4.41*				
			I Am Most Intimate With:					
A Man (N=48)				33.5				
A Woman (N=43)				30.2				
Jesus or God (N=60)				33.1				
Other (N=25)				31.6				
F-ratio				3.77*				

Note: * $p < .01$; ** $p < .05$.

Factor	Intergenerational Intimacy	Intergenerational Individuation	Intergenerational Intimidation	Intergenerational Triangulation	Peer Intimacy	Peer Individuation	Personal Authority	Theological Attitude
			I Can Feel Most Intimate With					
Seminarian (N=36)	83.2						41.5	38.2
Friend Outside (N=69)	90.9						46.7	38.2
Brother/Sister (N=10)	88.0						41.3	40.5
Mom or Dad (N=8)	101.0						47.1	34.1
Jesus or God (N=53)	93.2						46.9	35.5
F-ratio	3.13**						3.11**	3.04**
			Decisive About Becoming A Priest					
Absolutely Sure (N=50)	95.7	33.5	37.2		47.9	34.1		
Sure (N=99)	89.4	32.4	36.1		46.3	32.6		
Unsure (N=28)	81.3	30.2	32.7		44.4	30.8		
Very Unsure (N=2)	99.0	38.0	38.5		47.0	34.0		
F-ratio	5.26*	2.96**	5.09*		2.75**	3.06**.		

Note: * $p < .01$; ** $p < .05$.

APPENDIX C

Factor	Intergenerational Intimacy	Intergenerational Individuation	Intergenerational Intimidation	Intergenerational Triangulation	Peer Intimacy	Peer Individuation	Personal Authority	Theological Attitude
Make A Promise Of Celibacy								
Perpetual (N=100)	94.0		36.9					35.0
Temporary (N=15)	87.8		33.9					36.8
None At All (N=37)	88.2		35.9					42.6
Don't Know (N=28)	81.6		33.5					38.5
F-ratio	4.95*		4.05*					18.61*

Note: * $p < .01$; ** $p < .05$.

Appendix D
Maturity, Theological Attitude, and Age and Regional Factors
(Significant Mean Differences on the PAFS–QVC and Theological Attitude Scale Scores)

Factor	Intergenerational Intimacy	Intergenerational Individuation	Intergenerational Intimidation	Intergenerational Triangulation	Peer Intimacy	Peer Individuation	Personal Authority	Theological Attitude
Group Mean Scores	90.4	32.4	35.9	32.2	46.5	32.7	45.5	37.2
Age								
< 30 Years				31.2				
> 30 Years				33.7				
F-ratio				9.87*				
Region								
Atlantic Provinces					34.4			36.5
Quebec					30.7			39.7
Ontario					34.0			35.5
Western Provinces					33.0			35.6
F-ratio					6.707*			6.554*

Note: * p < .01.

APPENDIX D

Factor	Intergenerational Intimacy	Intergenerational Individuation	Intergenerational Intimidation	Intergenerational Triangulation	Peer Intimacy	Peer Individuation	Personal Authority	Theological Attitude
Theological Year								
First								35.2
Second								35.5
Third								38.4
Pastoral								40.0
Fourth								39.7
Fifth								36.5
F-ratio								3.82*

Note: * $p < .01$.

Appendix E
Maturity, Theological Attitude and Ethnic Factors
(Mean PAFS–QVC Scale and Theological Attitude Scale Scores and Ethnic Groups of Seminarians)

Factor	Intergenerational Intimacy	Intergenerational Individuation	Intergenerational Intimidation	Intergenerational Triangulation	Peer Intimacy	Peer Individuation	Personal Authority	Theological Attitude
Group Mean Scores	90.4	32.4	35.9	32.2	46.5	32.7	45.5	37.2
			Ethnic Group					
French Can. (N=58)	92.5	33.2	36.3	33.2	47.3	31.8	47.2	38.5
English Can. (N=30)	86.8	33.2	36.2	32.1	44.9	33.0	44.9	36.3
Canadian (N=14)	89.0	31.4	35.7	30.3	46.5	33.7	45.3	36.4
European (N=27)	89.5	31.7	36.5	33.4	48.1	35.9	45.0	35.5
Italian (N=7	93.1	33.7	35.9	30.0	41.6	32.6	46.3	32.0
Asian (N=7)	86.7	27.3	33.7	28.1	42.7	32.0	35.3	34.6
Other (N=7)	100.4	35.9	38.1	33.6	46.5	34.4	48.7	33.9
F-ratio	1.098	2.861	.710	2.418	2.728	2.530	2.185	2.167
F-probability	.37	.01	.64	.03	.02	.02	.05	.05

Glossary

Differentiation – a life–long process of striving to preserve self in close relationships; similar in meaning to individuation.

Enmeshment – also called "fusion"; blurred boundaries and little interpersonal distance; one's beliefs, attitudes, emotions and reactions are governed by the emotional aspects of close relationships.

Family of Origin – "the family in which a person has his/her beginnings – physiologically, psychically, and emotionally" (Hovestradt, Anderson, Piercy, Cochran, and Fine 1985, 287). This is the family in which one grew or with whom one spent most of one's childhood days.

Fusion (see *Enmeshment*)

Individuation – "is observed by an individual's ability to function in an autonomous and self–directed manner without being controlled, impaired, or feeling unduly responsible for significant others" (Williamson 1991, 275). Peer individuation is defined as the degree to which a person operates in an individuated, or, alternatively, fused, manner with significant others in his/her life.

Intimacy – "Intimacy may be defined as 'closeness with distinct boundaries'" (Lewis, Beavers, Gossett and Phillips 1976: Williamson 1981, 1982b, 310). Intergenerational intimacy is defined as the ability to be close, honest and loving to parents without undue enmeshment. Peer intimacy is defined as voluntary closeness to significant others in one's life, combined with distinct boundaries between oneself and them.

Intimidation – Intergenerational intimidation has been defined as the degree to which an individual yields to the wishes of his/her parents.

Mean – the sum of all scores divided by the number of scores; the average.

Personal Authority – a "synthesizing construct connecting individuation and intimacy" (Williamson 1991, 7). Personal authority has been described as the ability to balance intimacy and individuation with parents and peers while avoiding triangles and minimizing intimidation. Higher levels of personal authority suggest greater *maturity* in an individual's behaviour. This has been documented in the theoretical writings of Boszormenyi–Nagy and Spark (1973), Framo (1976, 1981), Bowen (1976, 1978), Kerr and Bowen (1988), and Williamson (1978, 1991), among others.

Scale – a group of questions designed to elicit responses which can then be graded or measured in terms of various factors of personal and social development; the range of possible responses.

Triangulation – Intergenerational triangulation is defined as being caught up in conflict between one's parents.

References

Bowen, M. 1976. Family therapy and family group therapy. In *Treating relationships,* edited by D. H. Olson. Lake Mills, Iowa: Graphic.
———. 1978. *Family therapy in clinical practice.* New York: Jason Aronson.
Bray, J. H., Williamson, D. and Malone, P. E. 1984a. Personal authority in the family system: Development of a questionnaire to measure personal authority in intergenerational family processes. *Journal of Marital and Family Therapy* 10:167–178.
———. *Personal authority in the family system questionnaire manual.* Houston: Houston Family Institute.
Bray, J. H. and Harvey, D. M. 1987. Intimacy and individuation in young adults: Development of the college student version of the Personal Authority in the Family System Questionnaire. Manuscript submitted for publication.
Bray, J. H. and Williamson, D. S. 1987a. Assessment of intergenerational relationships. In *Family–of–origin therapy: Applications in clinical practice,* edited by A. J. Hovestradt and M. Fine, Family Therapy Collections. Rockville, MD: Aspen Press.
———. Intergenerational family relationships: An evaluation of theory and measurement. *Psychotherapy* 24:516–528.
Canadian Conference of Catholic Bishops. 1991. Statistics of the Catholic Church in Canada. Ottawa: CCCB.

Canadian Conference of Catholic Bishops. 1992. Report of the Working Committee on the Selection and Formation of Candidates for the Priesthood. The Ad Hoc Committee on Sexual Abuse. Ottawa: CCCB.

DiNunzio, K. A. 1992. The self–assessments of career relationships in the family of origin and styles of managing work relationships. Dissertation; Temple University.

Douziech, R. 1994. Guardedness on the MMPI–2 in seminarian assessments. Unpublished raw data.

Euart, S. 1994. Transition time toward 21st century. *Origins* 23:770–776.

Gilligan, C. 1982. *In a different voice: Psychological theory and women's development.* Cambridge, Mass.: Harvard University Press.

Godin, A. 1983. *The psychology of religious vocations.* Washington: University Press of America.

Greeley, A. M. 1972a. The Catholic priest in the United States: Sociological investigations. Washington, D.C.: United States Catholic Conference.

———. 1972b. *Priests in the United States: Reflections on a survey.* New York: Doubleday Company.

Hemrick, E. F. and Hoge, D. R. 1985. Seminarians in theology: A national profile. Washington, D.C.: United States Catholic Conference.

———. 1987. Seminary life and the vision of the priesthood: A national survey of seminarians. Washington, D.C.: National Catholic Education Association.

———. 1991. A survey of priests ordained five to nine years. Washington, D.C.: The National Catholic Education Association.

Hoge, R., Potvin, R. and Ferry, K. M. 1984. Research on men's vocations to the priesthood and the religious life. Washington, D.C.: United States Catholic Conference.

Hoge, D. R., Shields, J. J. and Verdieck, M. J. 1988. Changing age distribution and theological attitudes of Catholic priests, 1970–1985. *Sociological analysis* 49:264–280.

Kerr, M. E. and Bowen, M. 1988. *Family evaluations: An approach based on Bowen theory.* New York: W. W. Norton & Company.

Kinnier, R. T., Brigman, S. L. and Noble, F. C. 1990. Career indecision and family enmeshment. *Journal of counselling and development* 68:309–311.

Krikorian, S. E. 1990. The relationship between level of differentiation from the family of origin and career decision–making among college students. Dissertation: California School of Professional Psychology, Los Angeles.

Laframboise, B. 1993. Finding voice: The psychological process of healing wounded women religious. Dissertation; University of Alberta.

Letter of the Doctrinal Congregation to the Bishops. 1986. The pastoral care of homosexual persons. *Origins* 16.

Lew, M. 1988. *Victims no longer: Men recovering from incest and other sexual child abuse.* New York: Harper & Row.

McBrien, J. A. 1992. Conflict in the church: Redefining the center. *America* 167: 78–81.

McGoldrick, M. and Gerson, R. 1985. *Genograms in family assessment.* New York: W. W. Norton.

Murphy, S. 1992. *A delicate dance: Sexuality, celibacy and relationships among Catholic clergy and religious.* New York: Crossroad.

National Opinion Research Center (NORC). 1972. The Catholic priest in the United States: Sociological investigations. Washington, D.C.: United States Catholic Conference.

Ohalloran, P. B. 1981. Bowen's concept of the differentiation of self and the Roman Catholic priesthood. Unpublished dissertation; University of Southern California.

Potvin, R. and Suziedelis, A. 1969. Seminarians in the sixties. Washington, D.C.: Center for Applied Research in the Apostolate (CARA).

Potvin, R. H. 1985. Seminarians of the eighties: A national survey. Washington, D.C.: National Catholic Education Association.

Rovers, Martin. 1995. Personal Authority in Roman Catholic Seminarians in Canada: A National Survey. Doctoral dissertation. Edmonton: University of Alberta.

Report of the Badgley Committee of Sexual Offenses Against Children

Stryckman, P. and Gaudet, R. 1971. Priests in Canada: A report on the English speaking clergy. Québec: Centre de Recherches en Sociologie Religieuse.

Stryckman, P. 1971. Les prêtres du Québec aujourd'hui. Québec: Centre de recherches en Sociologie Religieuse.

Sullender, R. S. 1993. Clergy candidates' MMPI profiles: Comparing gender and age variables. *The journal of pastoral care* 47:263–275.

Williamson, D. S. 1978. New life at the graveyard: A method of therapy for individuation from a dead former parent. *Journal of marriage and family counselling* 4:93–102.

———. 1981. Termination of the intergenerational hierarchical boundary between first and second generations: A new stage for the family. *Journal of marital and family therapy* 7:441–452.

———. 1982a. Personal authority in family experiences via termination of the intergenerational hierarchical boundary: Part II: The consultation process and the therapeutic method. *Journal of marital and family therapy* 8:23–38.

———. 1982b. Personal authority in family experiences via termination of the intergenerational hierarchical boundary; Part III: Personal authority defined and the power of play in the change–process. *Journal of marital and family therapy* 8:309–323.

———. 1991. *The intimacy paradox: Personal authority in the family system.* New York: The Guilford Press.

Williamson D. S. and Bray, J. H. 1988. Family development and change across the generations: An international perspective. In *Family transitions*, edited by C. J. Falicov, 357–384. New York: The Guilford Press.

Young, L. A. and Schoenherr, R. A. 1992. The changing age distribution and theological attitudes of Catholic priests revisited. *Social Analysis* 53:73–87.